Compatible with all air

Our recipes aim for universal compatibility with the myriad air fryer brands, Woodfire Outdoor Grill. Depending on your model's specifics and the dish's variables, slight adjustments may be needed, so embrace a little trial and error for optimal results. Our curated global recipes are chosen for their simplicity in an air fryer. Adhere to the guidelines as best you can, tweaking temperature and timings as required. **If your device has multiple other functions, such as grill, bake, roast, and so on, focus solely on the air fry or air crisp mode.**

Measurements and Regional Variations

Wherever feasible, we utilise a blend of familiar measurements: cups, teaspoons (tsp), tablespoons (tbsp), pounds (lb), ounces (oz), grams (g), kilograms (kg), millilitres (ml), litres (l), inches, millimetres (mm), and centimetres (cm). We use Fahrenheit (F) and Celsius (C) for temperature units. Always opt for level spoonfuls, not heaped. When referring to baking or roasting tins, air fryer cake barrels can often easily replace those, with the benefit of handles.

Spoon sizes and other measurements may vary globally. Whether metric or imperial, not all are identical. However, don't stress about matching measurements exactly. Use your available utensils and follow our recipes. Minor variations in quantity may occur due to regional differences, but remember, cooking thrives on flexibility and creativity!

Languages

Considering regional variations, we refer to the names and types of certain ingredients. For instance, what is known as aubergine in many regions is referred to as an eggplant in others. The same goes for plain flour, known elsewhere as all-purpose flour, which we simply write as flour in this publication, among other foods and ingredients. We strive to include alternative names for the same or similar items wherever possible.

Based in Cheshire, England, we use British English, leading to variations like 'flavour' over 'flavor'. Despite these regional language nuances and ingredient names, we strive for accessibility in our recipes. We choose widely available ingredients, often suggesting similar alternatives. Embrace the culinary journey!

Preheating

Most air fryers typically begin with a preheating phase, which can be frustrating for many individuals who do not want or require preheating for their meals.

Why Preheat

Preheating an air fryer before cooking offers several advantages. Firstly, it enhances cooking performance by ensuring the air fryer reaches the desired temperature, enabling immediate and even cooking. This results in improved texture and taste of the food. Additionally, it helps achieve a crispy exterior on food items, providing a crunch.

Preheating also contributes to food safety by quickly eliminating bacteria and pathogens during cooking. It maintains a consistent cooking temperature, preventing overcooking or undercooking. Preheating can be more energy-efficient, allowing the air fryer to cook food efficiently and effectively. Following the manufacturer's instructions regarding preheating times and temperatures for your specific air fryer model is recommended.

For ease, all our recipes in this publication require preheating unless suggested otherwise in any particular recipe.

If your air fryer does not have the option to preheat, switch on the air fryer to the temperature at which you intend to cook your food or according to the recipe method instructions, and increase the cooking time by 3 minutes. Start the air fryer, and after 3 minutes, your air fryer has been preheated. Certain air fryers have a light that turns off once the unit reaches the desired temperature. You should aim for this desired temperature when preheating.

Turning Off Preheat

It is generally advisable to assume that the air fryer should be allowed to preheat. When in doubt, it's recommended to preheat. If you wish to skip it, here is some advice.

Most air fryers automatically initiate a preheating process before prompting you to add the food once preheating is complete. However, not all air fryers have a dedicated button or method for selecting to disable preheating. While there is usually a way to accomplish these tasks, it is not always clearly indicated.

Stopping the preheating process on some models, when no specific stop option is available can often be as simple as holding the stop/start button for a few seconds. However, this may not be the case for all models. The same may apply to other brands, but the best way to determine this is by thoroughly reading the manual. If there is an option to override or enable preheating, it will most likely be mentioned in the manual.

A selection of popular quick cooks

Meats	Temperature	Time
Bacon	360F/180C	8-12
Burgers/Patties (1/4lb 114g)	360F/180C	8-12
Chicken (3lb8oz 1.6kg)	360F/180C	45-60
Chicken Breasts	360F/180C	8-12
Chicken Legs/Drumsticks	400F/200C	15
Chicken Thighs	400F/200C	10-16
Chicken Breast Strips	360F/180C	8-12
Chicken Wings	360F/180C	14-16
Fillet Steak (8oz 225g)	400F/200C	18
Lamb Chops	400F/200C	8-12
Meatballs	400F/200C	5-8
Pork Chops	400F/200C	15
Pork Loin (Whole)	360F/180C	18-21
Rack of Lamb	370F/190C	22
Ribeye Steak	400F/200C	12
Pork Ribs	400F/200C	10-15
Silverside	400F/200C	10-15
Sausages	400F/200C	15
Sirloin/New York Strip	400F/200C	9-14
Tenderloin	360F/180C	15

Vegetables	Temperature	Time
Asparagus	400F/200C	5-7
Beetroots/Beets	400F/200C	40
Broccoli Florets	400F/200C	6
Brussels Sprouts (Halves)	370F/190C	15
Carrots Sliced	360F/180C	15
Cauliflower Florets	400F/200C	12-15
Corn on the Cob	370F/190C	8
Aubergine/Eggplant slices	400F/200C	15
Green Beans	400F/200C	6-8
Mushrooms	400F/200C	5
Onions	400F/200C	10
Peppers (Bell)	370F/190C	10
Pepper Chunks (Bell)	370F/190C	8
Potato		
Baby	400F/200C	15
Wedges	400F/200C	15
Diced	400F/200C	12
Whole	400F/200C	45
Butternut Squash Chunks	400F/200C	2
Sweet Potatoes	370F/190C	30-35
Cherry Tomatoes	400F/200C	5
Courgette/Zucchini	400F/200C	12

Frozen Food	Temperature	Time
Cheese Sticks	370F/190C	10
Chicken Nuggets	370F/190C	10
Fish Fillets	370F/190C	10
Fish Fingers	370F/190C	15
Fries/Chips (Thick)	400F/200C	20
French Fries (Thin)	400F/200C	15
Spring Rolls	400F/200C	15-20

Seafood	Temperature	Time
Calamari/Squid	400F/200C	6
Fish Fillets	400F/200C	10-12
Salmon Fillets	360F/180C	8-12
Scallops	400F/200C	6-8
Prawns/Shrimp	360F/180C	6-8
Tuna Steak	400F/200C	8-12

Snacks and Desserts	Temperature	Time
Baked Apples	400F/200C	15
Banana Bread	360F/180C	25
Brownies	350F/170C	30
Cake (Whole)	360F/180C	20-25
Biscuits/Cookies	300F/150C	10
Muffins (Large)	370F/190C	15-20
Cupcakes	360F/180C	15
Pastries	350F/170C	10-12
Pizza for One	400F/200C	10-15
Quiche (Whole)	360F/180C	25-30

To make it easier to manage the settings on your air fryer, temperatures are rounded to approximate whole numbers. However, it's important to note that cooking times are also approximate and may vary depending on the texture and amount of food and the air fryer's model and make.

You should check on the food regularly when you cook it for the first time in your air fryer to ensure it's cooked to your liking. You may need to adjust the cooking times, ingredients, weights, and measurements to suit your preferences.

Batter splatter

It's a widespread belief that wet batter is unsuitable for an air fryer due to the potential for splattering induced by the high-speed circulating air. However, with a few clever techniques, you can sidestep this problem. If you find it challenging to achieve consistency in wet batter recipes, these tips could prove invaluable. You may even find it a fun exercise to innovate ways to thwart batter splatter.

Firstly, it's worth noting that not all air fryers have difficulty keeping batter attached to the food during cooking. If you find your air fryer tends to dislodge the batter before it sets, consider slightly reducing the temperature and extending the cooking time. Often, a lower cooking temperature maintained for a longer period can yield excellent results. Furthermore, to mitigate batter splatter, try attaching a sheet of tin foil to the top of a rack placed above the food. This will shield your dish from the brunt of the hot circulating air.

Step One: Thicker Batter. Prepare the thickest batter possible for the recipe at hand. If the batter seems too runny, gradually add flour and stir until you achieve the desired viscosity. With experience, you'll master the art of using batter in your air fryer and come to relish the process. Immerse your food in the batter, placed in a suitable container, and refrigerate it for 30 minutes. Periodically shaking the container will encourage the batter to infiltrate the food's nooks and crannies.

Step Two: Extract each food item from the container and, while the batter remains thick and sticky, gently cover them with dry flour by rolling or flipping them. Afterwards, lightly spritz each piece with cooking spray, vegetable, or olive oil. Then, return the food items to the refrigerator on a plate or dish until you're ready to cook them. It's advisable to prepare battered food well in advance of your meal.

Step Three: Once your food has been battered, floured, and oiled, arrange it in the air fryer basket and follow the recipe's cooking instructions. If time allows, lower the temperature and cook for slightly longer until your food achieves the desired look and degree of doneness, as per the recipe.

Popular conversions

Spoon, Cups & Liquids

1/4 tsp	1.25ml
1/2 tsp	2.5ml
1 tsp	5 ml
1 tbsp	15 ml
1/4 cup	60 ml
1/3 cup	80 ml
1/2 cup	125 ml
1 cup	250 ml

Temperatures

280 F	140 C
300 F	150 C
320 F	160 C
360 F	180 C
380 F	190 C
400 F	200 C
420 F	220 C
450 F	230 C

Dry Measurements

1 oz	28 g
2 oz	56 g
3 oz	85 g
4 oz	113 g
8 oz	226 g
12 oz	340 g
16 oz	454 g
32 oz	907 g

Popular Ingredients

1 Cup Flour	120 g
1 Cup Butter	220 g
1 Cup White Sugar	200 g
1 Cup Brown Sugar	220 g

To simplify things, the weights and measures provided are approximate and rounded off to remove decimals. Additionally, it is important to note that there may be ingredient variations due to differences in manufacturing or suppliers.

Which air fry?

Air fryers are fantastic kitchen devices, allowing you to swiftly and effortlessly create delicious and more nutritious renditions of your beloved fried foods. Instead of submerging the food in oil, an air fryer deploys hot air for cooking.

This technique yields a crispy and crunchy consistency without excessive fats and calories. Moreover, air fryers generally use less energy than traditional cooking techniques, making them efficient and economical. From traditional French fries to fried fish, chicken, and vegetables, an air fryer accommodates a variety of dishes.

What size?

The air fryer's suitable size depends on how much food you plan to cook. For instance, a compact air fryer with a 2 quart / 2.3-liter capacity should be adequate if you cook for a small family of one or two people. However, a larger air fryer ranging from 5 to 7 quarts / 5.5 to 8 liters might be better if you aim to make meals for a bigger family or entertain guests. Since the air fryer's size dictates the food quantity it can handle at once, it's essential to consider your usage needs before buying.

How to clean?

Cleaning an air fryer is a simple task with a few uncomplicated steps. Start by turning off and unplugging the air fryer, then remove any remaining food particles or debris from the basket. Next, take a damp cloth and wipe down the basket, lid, and the outer components of the fryer. If needed, a gentle detergent can help remove any stubborn residues. Once all surfaces are clean, use a dry cloth to dry the fryer thoroughly. Lastly, reassemble the air fryer and plug it in for your next use.

Safety?

- Always review the instruction manual of your air fryer before its initial use.
- Place the air fryer on a flat, stable surface, away from flammable materials.
- Avoid overfilling the basket.
- Use oven mitts when handling hot air fryer components.
- Keep the air fryer out of reach of children and pets.
- Unplug the air fryer when not in use.
- Inspect the air fryer's cords and plugs for any signs of damage.
- Employ the appropriate amount and type of cooking oil recommended by the manufacturer.
- Never leave the air fryer unattended during operation.
- Before each use, examine the air fryer and its surroundings for potential issues.

Interesting air fryer points

Safe to use

Air frying employs a convection process, where hot air circulates the food, resulting in a crispy outer layer while maintaining a tender interior. It's perfect for individuals looking for a healthier option than traditional frying, as air frying can replicate the texture of deep-fried food while using minimal oil.

Reduced harmful compounds

When specific foods are cooked at elevated temperatures using various cooking methods, they can generate harmful substances such as acrylamide, heterocyclic amines, and polycyclic aromatic hydrocarbons. Consumption of these substances can pose health risks to humans, including rare cancer cases. Thus, it's important to recognize that cooking any food at high temperatures using any cooking technique can form these substances.

- While meat plays a significant role, other foods cooked at high heat can also produce these compounds. Research suggests air frying might decrease acrylamide levels by up to 90%.

- Studies indicate that air frying could reduce the presence of potential cancer-causing compounds like heterocyclic amines. However, as cooking duration and temperature rise, the likelihood of these compounds forming also increases.

- The central point is that using an air fryer to rapidly cook food at high temperatures could be a healthier alternative than using a conventional oven and extended cooking times. However, it's crucial to be mindful of the convenience air fryers offer, which could lead to increased cooking frequency. Therefore, it's advisable to limit daily usage.

Energy saving

Even though air fryers are more energy-efficient than traditional cooking methods, some people might use them more frequently throughout the day, increasing energy consumption. To calculate the daily kWh (kilowatt hours) usage, you can multiply the wattage of a small air fryer (e.g., 1000 watts) by the number of hours it's been used. For example, if the air fryer has been used for 3 hours, the total wattage would be 3000, so dividing it by 1000 equals 3 kWh.

While this simple calculation can be done mentally, it's useful for appliances with varying wattages. Afterwards, the consumed kWh can be compared to what would have been used if traditional kitchen appliances like an oven were used, helping determine energy savings. Despite these potential savings, it's important to note that air frying has been scientifically validated as a healthy cooking method.

Weight loss

Air frying employs hot air to cook food and is frequently promoted as a healthier substitute for traditional deep frying, primarily because it uses less cooking oil. Consequently, air-fried foods may have lower calorie and fat contents. It's important to note that the health advantages of air frying can vary based on the ingredients and cooking methods used. For instance, preparing processed frozen foods with high salt, sugar, and artificial additives might not yield healthy results, unlike utilizing the air fryer for cooking fresh vegetables.

Food rotation

While using a microwave or conventional oven, we typically trust the timer to signal when the food is done. Yet, with an air fryer, it's essential to intermittently inspect and turn the food while cooking to ensure uniform hot air circulation. This practice guarantees even cooking.

Air fryer recipes

STARTERS

Bacon Wrapped Asparagus		1
Bacon Wrapped Pineapple		2
Blooming Onion		3
Brie Bites		4
Cheesy Potato Balls		5
Crispy Pork Belly		6
Devilled Eggs		7
Devils On Horseback		8
Pigs In A Blanket/Pastry		9
Pigs In Blankets/Kilted Soldiers		10
Pineapple Skewers		11
Pumpkin Soup		12
Sweet Potato Cheese Boats		13

MEAT & FISH

Beef

Bacon Wrapped Filet Mignon	
Beef Wellington	
Roast Beef	

Lamb

Boneless Lamb	
Lamb Chops	
Lamb Shanks	
Rack Of Lamb	

Pork

Gammon Joint	
Gammon Steaks	
Honey Sugar Ham	
Pork Tenderloin	
Honey Chili Pork Tenderloin	
Roast Pork	
Toad In The Hole	

Fish & Seafood

Breaded Scallops	
Honey Halibut	
Lobster Tails	
Salmon	

Poultry

Cornish Hens	
Duck Breasts	
Sticky Turkey Meatloaf	

14		
15		
16		
17		
18		
19		
20		
21		
22		
23		
24		
25		
26		
27		
28		
29		
30		
31		
32		
33		
34		

Stuffed Chicken & Bacon		35
Turkey Croquettes		36
Turkey Crown		37
Turkey Steaks		38
Whole Chicken		39
Whole Pheasant		40

FULL-PAGE SIDES

Brussels Sprouts & Chestnuts	41
Cauliflower Cheese	42
Dinner Rolls	43
Garlic Butter Mushrooms	44
Green Bean Casserole	45
Hasselback Potatoes	46
Marmite or Vegemite Roast Potatoes	47
Mashed Potatoes	48
Mixed Roasted Vegetables	49
Pork Stuffing Balls	50
Potato Gratin	51
Potato Salad	52
Roast Potatoes	53
Stuffed Mushrooms	54
Stuffing Balls	55
Traditional Stuffing	56
Yorkshire Puddings	57

HALF-PAGE SIDES

Cabbage	58
Crispy Cauliflower	58
Crispy Red Cabbage	59
Fried Green Beans	59
Fried Leeks	60
Fried Onions	60
Garlic Broccoli	61
Honey Parsnips	61
Red Roast Potatoes	62
Roasted Tinned/Canned Potatoes	62
Sweet Potato Chunks	63
Savoury Chunks	63
Traditional Roasted Chestnuts	64
Turnip Fries/Chips	64

DESSERTS

Apple Crumble	65	Pavlova	75
Apple Pie	66	Pecan Pie	76
Bread Pudding	67	Pumpkin Pie	77
Christmas Fruit Cake	68	Pumpkin Shakarparas	78
Christmas Victoria Sponge	69	Roasted Mixed Nuts	79
Gingerbread Men	70	Scones	80
Lemon Drizzle Cake	71	Shortbread Biscuits/Cookies	81
Melting Moments	72	Sugar Cookies/Biscuits	82
Mince Pies	73	Sweet Almonds	83
Nut Loaf	74	Sweet Pecans	84

Non-air fryer sauces, dips and gravy

After compiling a wonderful collection of recipes spanning starters, sides, desserts, and more, adding some non-air fryer sauces, dips, and more would be delightful.

As air frying can often leave little in the way of meat juices or fats, our meat gravies are meat juices and meat fats-free. However, if you find some meat juices and fats, feel free to add up to 30 ml/2 tbsp to the meat gravies. You can also adjust these items to suit your pallet.

Sauce / Gravy

Apple Sauce	85	Beef Gravy	90
Bechamel Sauce	85	Easy Gravy	91
Bread Sauce	86	KFC-Style Gravy	91
Cheese Sauce	86	Mushroom Gravy	92
Cranberry Sauce	87	Onion Gravy	92
Diane Sauce	87	Pork Gravy	93
Horseradish Cream Sauce	88	Turkey Gravy	93
Lemon Garlic Butter Sauce	88	Vegan Gravy & Gluten Free	94
Mint Sauce	89	Vegetable Gravy	94
Salted Caramel Sauce	89		
Seafood Sauce	90		

RECIPE NOTES

- To emphasise, each recipe utilises the "AIR FRY" or "AIR CRISP" setting on your appliance, not "BAKE", "ROAST", or any other modes your device may offer.
- All recipes require preheating the air fryer unless stated otherwise in the recipe.
- "Milk" means milk of choice unless otherwise stated in the recipe. Vegan milk may be used as a substitute if it closely matches the cookability of whole milk.
- "Butter" refers to your butter of choice unless otherwise stated in the recipe.
- Sea salt is our preferred choice, but you may use a salt you like.
- Olive oil is our preferred choice, but you may use an oil you like.
- "Spray oil" can be any cooking oil you choose, although we use olive oil.
- Some recipes have had ingredients and methods tweaked to optimise results when using the air fryer.
- For those utilising Ninja's Woodfire Grill & Smoker, the setup is as follows:
  Dial: Set to "AIR FRY" or "AIR CRISP," set the temperature and timer as per the recipe, and press "START/STOP".
  If you wish to add a smoky flavour to your air-fried dish, follow these steps: Pellets: Add your chosen pellets to the smoker box. Dial: Set to "AIR FRY" or "AIR CRISP," select "WOODFIRE FLAVOUR," set the temperature and timer per the recipe, and press "STOP/START."
- Air fryers may have different wattages and may cook at different speeds due to fan speeds, space inside the air fryer, quality of foods, volume and temperature of foods, and so on, so you might need to adjust the timer or temperature for the best results.

Bacon Wrapped Asparagus

12 thin-cut bacon rashers/slices			Asparagus		450 g	1 lb
Butter, melted	30 g	1 oz	Brown sugar		10 g	1 tbsp
Sea salt		1/4 tsp	Ground black pepper			1/4 tsp
12 toothpicks/cocktail sticks, soaked in water to help stop them burning or looking chard during cooking							

About

The culinary practice of wrapping vegetables in bacon is an age-old tradition that crosses many cultures, each with its unique twist. While it's hard to trace a single lineage for bacon-wrapped asparagus, its current popularity is a testament to how well these two ingredients combine, bringing the best of both worlds to Christmas tables.

Method

Divide the asparagus spears between the 12 rasher/slices of bacon, wrap the bacon around the bundles, and secure the bacon with a toothpick/cocktail stick. Combine the melted butter, brown sugar, salt, and pepper in a small bowl. Brush the mixture onto each asparagus bundle.

Place the bundles into the air fryer basket/tray/rack and cook at 200C/400F for 8 minutes or until the bacon is cooked and the asparagus is fork-tender. Once done, remove the bundles and serve. Repeat with any remaining bundles.

Serves 4 to 6, Preparation time approx 20 mins, Cooking time approx 8 mins

Bacon Wrapped Pineapple

8 rashers/slices of bacon			Chilli powder		1 tsp
1 pineapple, peeled, sliced lengthways			Toothpicks or cocktail sticks		
Brown sugar	45 g	1/4 cup			

About

Though it may not be a Christmas staple everywhere, bacon-wrapped pineapple has become a holiday treat in certain settings due to its flavour profile, aesthetic appeal, and the joyful social interaction it can foster. The dish often looks quite festive, with the bright yellow of the pineapple and the rich colour of the bacon presenting an eye-catching addition to the Christmas table.

Method

In a small bowl, mix brown sugar and chilli powder. Wrap each pineapple length with a bacon slice, securing it with a toothpick/cocktail stick. Coat the bacon-wrapped pineapple in the sugar chilli mixture.

Cook the wedges in the air fryer basket/tray/rack without overcrowding at 200C/400F for 12 to 15 minutes, flipping halfway through until the bacon is crispy and the pineapple is tender.

Serves 4, Preparation time approx 30 mins, Cooking time approx 15 mins

Blooming Onion

1 large onion			Onion powder		1 tsp
Plain/all-purpose flour	120 g	1 cup	Sea salt		1/2 tsp
Garlic powder		1 tsp	Ground black pepper		1/2 tsp
Paprika		1 tsp	Beer of choice	125 ml	1/2 cup
Panko or coarse breadcrumbs	30 g	1/4 cup			

About

Blooming onions can make a delightful addition to your Christmas festivities. These air-fried onion "flowers" are visually appealing and offer a scrumptious and somewhat novel treat for your holiday table.

Method

Peel and top the onion, then cut it into segments from the top without cutting all the way through to create a blooming onion shape. Mix flour, garlic powder, paprika, onion powder, salt, and pepper in a bowl.

In a separate bowl, whisk beer and panko breadcrumbs. Dip the onion in the flour mixture, then the beer mixture, and back into the flour mixture for a thorough coating. Cook in the air fryer basket/tray/rack at 180C/360F for 10 minutes.

Serves 2, Preparation time approx 30 mins, Cooking time approx 10 mins

Brie Bites

Brie cheese	225 g	8 oz	Plain/all-purpose	60 g	1/2 cup
1 egg, beaten			Milk	15 ml	1 tbsp
Panko or coarse breadcrumbs	100 g	1 cup			

About

Brie is one of the oldest known cheeses, dating back over 1,200 years to France. Dubbed the "Queen of Cheeses," brie was said to have been a favourite of Charlemagne, the first Holy Roman Emperor. The notion of appetisers or hors d'oeuvres became popular in Western culinary traditions in the 19th and 20th centuries. These bite-sized portions are served before main courses and at seasonal celebrations.

Method

Cut brie into cubes of roughly 2.5 cm/1-inch. Arrange three bowls: one with flour, another with a mix of egg and milk, and the third with breadcrumbs. Dip each brie cube in flour, then the egg mixture, and then coat with breadcrumbs. Arrange the coated cubes on a tray in a single layer and place them in the freezer for 1 hour so that you are cooking from frozen so that the bites hold their shape while cooking.

Line the air fryer basket/tray/rack with parchment paper. Cook at 200C/400F for 8 minutes or until they turn golden. Garnish and serve with dips (optional)

Serves 2, Preparation time approx 1 hour 30 mins, Cooking time approx 8 mins

Cheesy Potato Balls

6 potatoes, peeled, chopped			Sea salt			1/2 tsp
Ground black pepper		1/4 tsp	6 bacon rashers/slices			
Butter	15 g	1 tbsp	Mature cheddar, grated/shredded	120 g	1 cup	
Mozzarella cheese, cubed	120 g	4 oz	3 spring onions, finely chopped			
Spray oil			White breadcrumbs	100 g	1 cup	
2 eggs, beaten			Garlic powder			1/2 tsp

About

The history of cheesy potato balls isn't documented, but they can be considered a part of the broader tradition of fritters, croquettes, and dumplings found in various cuisines worldwide. Nevertheless, they add a nice touch at Christmas.

Method

Half-fill a saucepan with water, season with the sea salt, and bring to a boil. Add the potatoes and boil them until soft. Cook the bacon in the air fryer basket/tray/rack at 200C/400F for 4 minutes, then finely chop it. Mash the boiled potatoes in a bowl with butter, salt, pepper, and garlic. Stir in the bacon, spring onion, and cheddar cheese. Chill this mixture in the fridge for at least an hour.

Whisk eggs in one bowl and add the breadcrumbs to another. Shape the chilled potato mixture into balls, inserting a mozzarella cube in each and coat them in the whisked egg, then the breadcrumbs. Chill in the fridge for 30 minutes. Lightly oil spray them and cook them in the air fryer basket/tray/rack at 190C/370F for 8 minutes or until golden.

Serves 4, Preparation time approx 45 mins, Cooking time approx 8 mins

Crispy Pork Belly

Pork belly, cut to 2.5 cm/1 inch cubes	450 g	1 lb	Olive oil	30 ml	2 tbsp
Garlic powder		1 tsp	Smoked paprika		1 tsp
Sea salt	10 g	2 tsp	Ground black pepper		1 tsp

About

Crispy belly pork, also known as pork belly, is a succulent and flavourful cut of meat adorned with a layer of fat that renders beautifully when cooked, resulting in tantalisingly crispy skin. Christmas is a time of indulgence, and pork belly's rich, fatty nature certainly fits the festive bill. The contrast between the crispy skin and tender meat provides a luxurious eating experience.

Method

Combine the olive oil, garlic powder, smoked paprika, sea salt, and pepper in a bowl. Thoroughly toss the pork cubes in the seasoning and rub it into the pork by hand. Cook at 190C/370F in the air fryer basket/tray/rack for 20 minutes or until golden and crispy, stirring the cubes every 5 minutes. Leave the cubes to rest for 5 minutes before serving to give them a chance to crisp up still further.

Serves 2 to 4, Preparation time approx 30 mins, Cooking time approx 20 mins

Devilled Eggs

6 large eggs			Dijon mustard	5 ml	1 tsp
Mayonnaise	30 ml	2 tbsp	Sea salt		1/4 tsp
Ground black pepper		1/4 tsp	Paprika for garnish		

About

While the concept of stuffing eggs has been around for centuries, the "devilled eggs" dish is rooted in European and American cuisines. Devilled eggs are a dish with ancient origins that have been adapted and reinterpreted through the years to suit changing culinary tastes and cultural influences. They remain a popular and versatile dish enjoyed across various occasions. Devilled eggs have a long-standing history as part of the Christmas feast. Continuing the tradition can evoke nostalgia and continuity.

Method

Cook the eggs in shells in the air fryer basket/tray/rack at 190C/370F for 12 minutes. Subsequently, plunge the cooked eggs into an ice-water bath for five minutes. Peel the eggs, slice them in half lengthwise, and carefully remove the yolks. Combine the yolks with mayonnaise, mustard, salt, and pepper, mashing them together to create the filling.

Pipe the yolk mixture into the hollowed-out egg whites using a piping or a plastic bag with a corner snipped off. Dust with paprika and return the filled eggs to the air fryer, cooking for an additional three minutes at 190C/370F. Garnish as desired.

Serves 3 to 6, Preparation time approx 15 mins, Cooking time approx 13 mins

Devils On Horseback

24 prunes, destoned			24 almonds		
12 rashers/slices of streaky bacon			Soy sauce	30 ml	2 tbsp
Honey	30 ml	2 tbsp	Ground black pepper		1/4 tsp
24 toothpicks/cocktail sticks, soaked in water to help stop them burning or looking chard during cooking					

About

While its exact roots are somewhat unclear, the dish is widely thought to be a variation of Angels on Horseback, an oyster-based hors d'oeuvre that dates back to the 19th century. This culinary treat has been a staple of celebrations and gatherings, including Christmas and New Year's Eve parties.

Method

Fill each prune with an almond, padding out the prunes. Remove any bacon rind/skin and slice the rashers/slices in half lengthwise to create thin strips. Wrap a bacon strip around each stuffed prune, securing it with a water-soaked cocktail stick.

Combine the honey, pepper, and soy sauce in a small bowl to create a glaze. Lightly coat each devil on horseback in the glaze and let excess drip off. Cook them in the air fryer basket/tray/rack at 200C/400F for 10 minutes or until the bacon is crispy.

Serves 4 to 6, Preparation time approx 45 mins, Cooking time approx 10 mins

Pigs In A Blanket/Pastry

Crescent dough or you can purchase premade crescent dough

Plain/all-purpose flour	360 g	3 cups	Granulated sugar	35 g	3 tbsp
Dry active yeast		2 tsp	Sea salt		1/2 tsp
Unsalted butter	225 g	8 oz	Milk	125 ml	1/2 cup
Water	60 ml	1/4 cup	2 eggs, beaten		

Pigs In A Blanket

Enough premade crescent pastry to wrap 20 sausages, cut into long triangles no wider than the sausages (or use the crescent dough recipe					
Spray oil			20 precooked or smoked mini sausages		

About

In recent years, serving "pigs in a blanket" or mini sausages wrapped in crescent roll dough has become a popular tradition during Christmas gatherings, New Year's Eve parties, and other festive occasions.

Method

Crescent dough: Whisk flour, sugar, yeast, and salt in a large bowl. Cut in butter until pea-sized pieces of dough form. Mix milk, water, and egg in a small bowl and add to the flour mixture a little at a time. Stir until the dough forms a ball. Wrap the dough in cling film/plastic wrap and refrigerate for 30 minutes. On a floured surface, roll the dough to half an inch thick. Fold it in thirds, rotate 90 degrees, and repeat 3 to 5 times. Refridgerate again for 30 minutes. Divide the dough into 3. Roll each into a 3 mm / 1/8-inch thick, 40 cm x 12 cm / 16 x 5-inch rectangle. Cut again into thin triangles, thin enough so the sausage pokes out.

Pigs in a blanket: Encase each cocktail or mini sausage with dough, starting at the wide end of the dough triangle and finishing at the point. Secure with a cocktail stick if needed. Lightly mist the dough with oil. Cook in the air fryer basket/tray/rack at 190C/370F for about 6 minutes or until the dough turns golden and is fully cooked.

Serves upto 10 at 2 each, Preparation time 30 mins, Cooking time approx 6 mins

Pigs In Blankets/Kilted Soldiers

20 cocktail sausages, or chipolatas			Spray oil		
10 slices of streaky bacon, cut in half			Toothpicks or cocktail sticks		
Honey	15 ml	1 tbsp			

About

The origin of pigs in blankets is somewhat murky, but wrapping meat in other meat is familiar. Various cultures have their versions of this dish. The sausages and bacon provide a satisfying, fatty richness that pairs wonderfully with other traditional Christmas foods. Furthermore, they are relatively easy to prepare in large quantities, making them an ideal choice for a feast meant to serve many people. Pigs In Blankets is different to Pigs In A Blanket, which encases the sausages in pastry, not bacon.

Method

Add the honey to a large bowl, then add the sausages and thoroughly coat them in the honey. With only 15 ml/1 tbsp of honey, getting it on every part of the sausage might be a little work, but it's worth the effort.

Wrap half a slice of bacon around each sausage and secure the bacon with toothpicks or cocktail sticks. Cook them at 200C/400F in the air fryer basket/tray/rack for 8 minutes, turning halfway through.

Serves 4 to 5, Preparation time approx 30 mins, Cooking time approx 8 mins

Pineapple Skewers

1 pineapple, peeled, core removed, cut into chunks					
Butter, melted	15 g	1/2 oz	Maple syrup	30 ml	2 tbsp
Ground cinnamon		1 tsp			
Enough wooden skewers to thread the chunks that will fit the basket/tray/rack. Soak the skewers in water for 30 minutes before use					

About

The popularity of pineapples during the Christmas season might initially seem odd, given its tropical origin. Still, it has deep-rooted historical and cultural significances that contribute to its festive association. The pineapple has long been a symbol of welcome, hospitality, and friendship in many cultures. Pineapple often accompanies Christmas ham. The sweetness of pineapple pairs well with the saltiness of ham, and this pairing has become a traditional Christmas dish in many households.

Method

Place the pineapple chunks in a large bowl. Blend the melted butter, maple syrup, and cinnamon in a separate bowl, then pour the mixture over the pineapple and stir together, ensuring the chunks are evenly coated.

Cook the chunks in a single layer in the air fryer basket/tray/rack at 200C/400F for 12 minutes or until the coating has caramelised, turning the slices halfway through. Serve either warm or cold, suitable as a side or dessert.

Serves 4 to 6, Preparation time approx 30 mins, Cooking time approx 12 mins

Pumpkin Soup

Chicken stock	500 ml	2 cups	Coarse sea salt		1/2 tsp
Ground nutmeg		1/4 tsp	Honey	15 ml	1 tbsp
Olive oil	30 ml	2 tbsp	Garlic powder		1/4 tsp
1 onion, peeled, quartered			Butternut squash/pumpkin, peeled	900 g	2 lb

About

The vibrant orange of pumpkin soup adds a festive touch to the Christmas dinner table, matching traditional Christmas decorations. Whether for the taste, the nutritional benefits, or the ease of preparation, pumpkin soup is special in Christmas celebrations.

Method

Cut the butternut into chunks of about 5 cm / 2 inches. Combine the honey, onion, garlic, and oil in a large bowl. Add the butternut and onion to the mixture and coat well. Cook the butternut and onion in the air fryer basket/tray/rack at 200C/400F for 10 minutes or until fork tender and slightly caramelised.

In an electric blender, fill to halfway and blend the vegetables and stock until smooth. Season the blended soup with a bit of salt and nutmeg. Portion the soup into individual bowls. Enhance with a swirl of sour/soured cream and a sprinkling of chives (optional). Serve at this slightly warm temperature, cold, or heat it hot.

Serves 4, Preparation time approx 45 mins, Cooking time approx 10 mins

Sweet Potato Cheese Boats

Desiccated coconut	45 g	1/2 cup	Coconut cream	150 ml	2/3 cup
Coconut oil	30 ml	2 tbsp	1 onion, peeled, finely chopped		
Fresh ginger, grated/shredded		1 tbsp	2 garlic cloves, grated/shredded		
4 medium-sized sweet potatoes					

About

Sweet potatoes have become a staple in many Christmas meals, especially in Western countries, and their popularity during the festive season can be attributed to a combination of historical, cultural, and culinary reasons. This dish can be a great starter, side, or main coarse.

Method

Mix desiccated coconut and coconut cream in a bowl, then set aside. Clean the sweet potatoes and pat dry. Pierce them with a fork in several places and cook in the air fryer basket/tray/rack at 290C/370F for 50 minutes or until fork tender, turning them occasionally for even cooking.

Make a single cut along the length of the potato or cut a section of the skin out entirely if they are irregular shapes. Scoop out most of their insides, leaving about 5 mm / 1/5 of the flesh lining the inside of the skin. In a large bowl, mash the scooped potato with coconut oil. Stir in the coconut mixture, onion, ginger, garlic, orange juice and zest.

Fill the potato skins with the mixture and cook in the air fryer basket/tray/rack at 200C/400F for 8 minutes or until thoroughly heated.

Serves 4, Preparation time approx 30 mins, Cooking time approx 1 hour

Bacon Wrapped Filet Mignon

4 filet mignon steaks			4 slices of bacon of choice		
Ground black pepper	1/2 tsp		Coarse sea salt		1/2 tsp
Spray oil					
4 toothpicks/cocktail sticks, soaked in water to help stop them burning or looking chard during cooking					

About

The tradition of serving bacon-wrapped filet mignon during Christmas festivities has various points of origin. Filet mignon is a cut of beef taken from the smaller end of the tenderloin and known for its tenderness and flavour. Christmas originated in the Christian tradition but is now celebrated more broadly and has long been associated with festive and luxurious feasting. In Western culture, red meat is often considered a luxury or special occasion food, making it a popular choice for celebrating Christmas.

Method

Wrap each filet mignon with a slice of bacon, securing it with a toothpick/cocktail stick. Pierce the toothpick through the bacon and edge of the filet, ensuring it exits through the bacon on the opposite side—season with salt and pepper.

Lightly oil spray the filets and cook them in the air fryer basket/tray/rack at 190C/370F for 10 minutes or until the meat has an internal temperature of 50C/120F rare, 60C/140F medium, and 70C/160F well-done. Turn them over halfway through cooking.

Serves 4, Preparation time approx 30 mins, Cooking time approx 10 mins

Beef Wellington

Beef tenderloin	700 g	1 1/2 lb	Sea salt		1/4 tsp
Olive oil	30 ml	2 tbsp	Ground black pepper		1/4 tsp
Liver pâté, smooth	170 g	6 oz	Dijon mustard	60 ml	1/4 cup
1 large sheet of puff pastry			1 egg, beaton		

About

Beef Wellington is a classic dish that is a popular choice for festive occasions, especially Christmas. Christmas is a time for indulgence, and Beef Wellington, with its premium ingredients, fits the bill perfectly.

Method

Season the beef with salt and pepper. Sear the meat in a frying pan/skillet with hot olive oil for 5 minutes or until browned. Rotate it every minute or so. Let it cool at room temperature before applying a layer of pâté by hand all over the beef. Next, add a thin layer of Dijon mustard. Roll out puff pastry to a thickness of about 5 mm / 1/5 inch on a lightly floured surface. Centre the beef on the pastry, wrapping and sealing it, trimming any excess. Brush the beaten egg over the pastry.

Cook at 190C/370F in the air fryer basket/tray/rack for 25 minutes or until the pastry is golden and the beef is cooked to your liking. For rare, the internal temperature must reach 50C/120F, 60C/140F for medium-rare, 65C/150F for medium, 70C/160F for medium-well done, or 80C/180F for well done.

Serves 4 to 6, Preparation time approx 1 hour, Cooking time approx 25 mins

Roast Beef

Beef for roasting of choice	1.4 kg	3 lb	Olive oil		30 ml	2 tbsp
Garlic powder		1 tsp	Smoked paprika			1 tsp
Worcestershire sauce	10 ml	2 tsp	Sea salt			1 tsp
Ground black pepper		1 tsp				

About

Enjoying roast beef, particularly during celebratory occasions, has deep historical roots in many cultures. Its appeal as a centrepiece for a Christmas feast can be attributed to a blend of historical precedent, gastronomic pleasure, and cultural affinity. The "Sunday roast", a weekly ritual in many households, often features roast beef as the main attraction. Given that Christmas dinner is an elaborate version of a Sunday roast, it's unsurprising that roast beef appears.

Method

Mix oil, garlic, paprika, Worcestershire sauce, salt and pepper in a large bowl. Brush the joint with the mixture and cook it in the air fryer basket/tray/rack at 190C/370F for 20 minutes per 450 g/1 lb. After 20 minutes, flip the joint and continue to cook until the internal temperature reaches 65C/150F. Allow it to rest for 10 minutes before slicing.

Serves 4 to 6, Preparation time approx 30 mins, Cooking time approx 50 mins

Boneless Lamb

1 boneless leg or shoulder of lamb, trimmed, tied				1.4 to 1.6 kg	3 to 3 1/2 lb
2 garlic cloves, grated/shredded			Olive oil	30 ml	2 tbsp
Dried rosemary		1 tbsp	Dried thyme		1 tsp
Sea salt		1 tsp	Ground black pepper		1/2 tsp
1 lemon, sliced					

About

The tradition of serving roast lamb at Christmas has historical and cultural roots that vary by region. While turkey and other fowls may dominate the Christmas tables in countries like the United Kingdom and the United States, roast lamb has its special place, particularly in various European traditions.

Method

Combine garlic, olive oil, rosemary, thyme, salt, and pepper in a bowl. Massage this mixture onto the lamb, ensuring it reaches into all crevices. Refrigerate the lamb for 30 minutes, then cook the lamb in the air fryer basket/tray/rack, topped with lemon slices at 190C/370F for 20 minutes per 450 g/1 lb of lamb, or until the internal temperature of the lambe is 65C/150F for medium-rare. Allow the lamb to rest before serving.

Serves 4 to 6, Preparation time approx 20 mins, Cooking time approx 1 hour

Lamb Chops

8 lamb chops			Olive oil	30 ml	2 tbsp
2 garlic cloves, grated/shredded			Dried rosemary		1 tsp
Dried thyme	1 tsp		Sea salt		1/2 tsp
Ground black pepper	1/2 tsp				

About

Including lamb chops in Christmas feasting has diverse roots and rationales, ranging from cultural traditions and historical contexts to culinary factors. In some cultures, lamb holds particular symbolic or religious significance, often associated with themes of renewal and sacrifice, which makes it a poignant choice for occasions like Christmas.

Method

In a large bowl, combine the olive oil, garlic, rosemary, thyme, salt, and pepper. Toss the chops in the mixture, thoroughly coating them. Cover the bowl and leave the chops to marinate in the mix in the fridge for an hour or up to 8 hours. Cook the chops at 200C/400F in the air fryer basket/tray/rack for 10 minutes for medium, or adjust the time to your preference. Flip them halfway through.

Serves 2 to 4, Preparation time approx 30 mins, Cooking time approx 10 mins

Lamb Shanks

2 lamb shanks			Olive oil	30 ml	2 tbsp
2 garlic cloves, finely grated			Dried oregano		1/2 tsp
Ground cumin		1/2 tsp	Ground black pepper		1/2 tsp
Sea salt		1/2 tsp	Freshly squeezed lemon juice	30 ml	2 tbsp
White wine	125 ml	1/2 cup	Tomato paste	30 ml	2 tbsp
Honey	30 ml	2 tbsp	Freshly chopped coriander/cilantro		1 tsp

About

While they may not have the long-standing Christmas associations that other meats like turkey or ham have, lamb shanks offer a sumptuous and increasingly popular alternative that can make the holiday meal memorable. As Christmas traditions evolve and merge due to globalisation, foods commonly associated with Christmas in one culture may be adopted by others.

Method

Combine the olive oil, garlic, oregano, cumin, pepper, and salt and season evenly over the shanks. Cook the shanks at 180C/360F in the air fryer basket/tray/rack for 45 minutes or until they are cooked. Fifteen minutes into the cooking, combine the remaining ingredients, brush them over the shanks and continue cooking for the last 15 minutes, or until the internal temperature of the shanks reaches at least 65C/150F. Garnish with any remaining sauce and chopped coriander/cilantro.

Serves 2, Preparation time approx 15 mins, Cooking time approx 45 mins

Rack Of Lamb

One French trimmed rack of lamb, large enough to fit the basket/tray/rack, 8 bones is typical, preferably fat on					
Olive oil	15 ml	1 tbsp	Dried rosemary		1 tsp
Dried thyme		1 tsp	Sea salt		1/2 tsp
Ground black pepper		1/4 tsp			

About

Serving a rack of lamb for Christmas dinner offers a delightful departure from traditional festive meats like turkey, ham, or beef. A rack of lamb is often considered a luxury item, making it fitting for a special occasion like Christmas. The meat is incredibly tender and flavourful, mainly when the rack is perfectly cooked.

Method

Mix olive oil, rosemary, thyme, salt, and pepper on a plate. Pat the lamb rack dry and coat thoroughly with the herb mixture. Cook in the air fryer basket/tray/rack for 15 minutes or until 60C/140F internal temperature for medium rare.

Extend cooking by a few minutes for a more well-done result. Once done, remove the lamb, cover with foil, and let rest for at least 10 minutes before serving.

Serves 4, Preparation time approx 15 mins, Cooking time approx 15 mins

Gammon Joint

1 gammon	900 g	2 lb	Brown sugar	20 g	2 tbsp
Maple syrup	30 ml	2 tbsp	Honey	30 ml	2 tbsp
Dijon mustard	30 ml	2 tbsp	Apple cider vinegar	30 ml	2 tbsp
2 garlic cloves, grated/shredded			Ground black pepper		1/4 tsp

About

Originally, the consumption of gammon at Christmas was closely tied to the agricultural calendar. In times when refrigeration was not available, pigs were often slaughtered in the late autumn or early winter. The meat would then be cured to be ready to eat by Christmas. In pre-Christian Europe, the Yule festival, which was celebrated during the winter solstice, often included the sacrifice and consumption of a boar. The Christian adoption of this became part of the Christmas feast.

Method

Combine all of the ingredients in a bowl other than the gammon. Score a crisscross or other pattern across the skin or a thick layer of fat, and cover the whole gammon with the glaze mixture. Cook in the air fryer basket/tray/rack at 180C/360F for 30 to 40 minutes or until the gammon is cooked to your liking and has reached an internal temperature of 68C/155F.

Serves 4 to 6, Preparation time approx 20 mins, Cooking time approx 40 mins

Gammon Steaks

2 thick gammon steaks			Honey		15 ml	1 tbsp
Olive oil		30 ml	2 tbsp	Dijon mustard (optional)	30 ml	2 tbsp

About

Gammon or ham? Gammon refers to the hind leg of pork that has been cured and comes from the hind leg. Gammon is typically sold raw and requires cooking. Ham typically refers to the hind leg of pork cured and then cooked or smoked. Therefore, when you buy a ham, it's generally ready to eat, although many people like to glaze and roast it to enhance its flavour. Gammon is a delicious seasonal treat.

Method

Create a glaze by blending the olive oil, mustard, and honey. Dry the ham or gammon steaks using paper towels and apply the glaze to both sides. Cook gammon steaks in the air fryer basket/tray/rack at 180C/360F for 5 minutes, flip and reapply the glaze.

Once the first 5 minutes are up and the gammon has been flipped and more glaze added, continue cooking for 5 minutes or until they reach an internal temperature of 65C/150F.

This recipe can be adapted to ham steaks by reducing the cooking time to 3 minutes per side, presuming the ham has been precooked or smoked, as is usually the case with ham.

Serves 2, Preparation time approx 15 mins, Cooking time approx 10 mins

Honey Sugar Ham

Cooked ham, bone-in or out	900 g	2lb	Brown sugar	90 g	1/2 cup
Honey sugar glaze					
Honey	60 ml	1/4 cup	Freshly squeezed orange juice	60 ml	1/4 cup
Apple cider vinegar	15 ml	1 tbsp	Ground cinnamon		1/4 tsp
Brown sugar	90 g	1/2 cup	Ground black pepper		1/4 tsp

About

In pre-refrigeration days, pigs were often prepared in late autumn or early winter, providing fresh meat that could be cured and ready by Christmas. The timing naturally led to the tradition of enjoying ham during Christmas.

Method

Remove the ham from the fridge an hour before cooking to reach room temperature. Prepare the glaze by combining the honey sugar glaze ingredients in a saucepan. Heat gently until the sugar dissolves, then set aside.

Remove netting from the ham and make 1.3 cm / 1/2 inch cuts/scores on the surface of the ham about 2.5 cm / 1 inch apart. Line the air fryer basket/tray/rack with overlapping foil sheets and place the ham on top. Brush with a third of the glaze, wrap tightly in foil, and cook at 170C/340F for 25 minutes.

Open the foil from the ham, apply more glaze, and reseal the foil. Cook for another 25 minutes at 170C/340F. Then, adjust the foil to create a 'boat' around the ham to retain liquid. Apply more glaze and air fry at 180C/360F for 5 minutes or until the glaze has caramelised. Remove the ham and let it rest for 10 minutes before slicing. Meanwhile, combine the remaining glaze with juices from the foil boat and simmer it in a saucepan until thickened, and either brush onto the ham or serve separately.

Serves 4 to 6, Preparation time approx 1 hour, Cooking time approx 1 hour.

Honey Chilli Pork Tenderloin

Pork tenderloin	700 g	1 1/2 lb	Spray oil			
Chilli powder		1/4 tsp	Sea salt			1/4 tsp
Smoked paprika		1/2 tsp	Garlic powder			1/2 tsp
Onion powder		1/2 tsp	Dried oregano			1/2 tsp
Ground black pepper		1/4 tsp	Olive oil		15 ml	1 tbsp
Honey	15 ml	1 tbsp				

About

As the name suggests, the tenderloin is one of the most tender cuts of pork, making it a prime choice for special occasions when serving a delicious and impressive meal is paramount. In some regions and families, serving pork during Christmas has become a cherished tradition passed down through generations.

Method

In a small bowl, combine the chilli, salt, paprika, garlic, onion powder, oregano, and black pepper. Lay the pork on a cutting board and cut it in half if it is too long for the air fryer. Brush it with olive oil, then evenly apply the spice mixture in a thin coating.

Cook the tenderloin in the air fryer basket/tray/rack at 200C/400C for 5 minutes. Afterwards, reduce the heat to 160C/320F and cook for 12 minutes or until the tenderloin reaches an internal temperature of 65C/150F. Remove from the air fryer, wrap it in foil, and leave it to rest for 15 minutes before slicing and serving.

Serves 4, Preparation time approx 30 mins, Cooking time approx 17 mins

Pork Tenderloin

Olive oil	15 ml	1 tbsp	Cayenne pepper		1/4 tsp
Garlic powder		1/2 tsp	Ground black pepper		1/2 tsp
Onion powder		1/2 tsp	Mustard powder		1/2 tsp
Sea salt		1 tsp	Pork tenderloin	700 g	1 1/2 lb
Brown sugar	10 g	1 tbsp			

About

Various factors, including regional traditions, personal preferences, and culinary considerations, can influence the choice of pork tenderloin for Christmas dinner. In some cultures and regions, pork is the meat for festive occasions, including Christmas.

Method

Combine the dry spices, salt and pepper in a bowl. Prepare the pork tenderloin by removing any excess fat or silver skin. Lightly coat the meat with 2 tsp of olive oil, then evenly apply the spice mixture over the entire surface of the tenderloin.

Cook the pork in the air fryer basket/tray/rack at 200C/400F for 20 minutes or until the internal temperature of the meat reaches 65C/150F. Once cooked, wrap the pork in foil and leave it to rest for 15 minutes before carving. Retain any juices that accumulate on the chopping board or in the foil, which can be drizzled over the meat or added to gravy.

Serves 4, Preparation time approx 30 mins, Cooking time approx 20 mins

Roast Pork

Pork, for roasting, ideally the loin, which is lean and requires less cooking, with rind/skin on	1.5 kg	3 lb 5 oz
Coarse sea salt	20 g	2 tbsp		

About

Pork is a succulent, flavourful meat that lends itself well to roasting. The meat's sweetness pairs wonderfully with various traditional Christmas sides, from applesauce to root vegetables, and even complements spicier offerings like stuffing. One of the highlights of roast pork is undoubtedly the crackling—crisp, salty, and incredibly moreish. Achieving perfect crackling is a culinary feat that many aspire to, and when done right, it can elevate the entire meal.

Method

Cut slits in the pork rind down through the fat layer, stopping before reaching the meat. Space these cuts about 5 mm / 1/5 inch apart for optimal crackling. Rub salt into these cuts, avoiding the meat on the sides and underneath, which should only be lightly sprinkled with salt. Allow the pork to rest in the fridge, uncovered, for two hours.

Cook the pork, rind side up, in the air fryer basket/tray/rack at 180C/360F for 45 minutes, adding a small amount of water to a dish underneath the basket, if there is room, or in a small but deep heat-proof dish, such as a ramakin dish next to the pork.

Finally, up the temperature to 200C/400F and cook the pork for a further 15 minutes or until the rind is crisp yet not burned and the internal temperature of the pork reaches at least 65C/150F. Leave the pork to rest for 30 minutes uncovered before slicing.

Serves 4 to 6, Preparation time approx 20 mins, Cooking time approx 40 mins

Toad In The Hole

4 to 6 thick pork sausages			Olive oil	30 ml	2 tbsp
2 large eggs			Plain/all-purpose flour	80 g	3/4 cup
Milk	225 ml	1/2 cup			

About

The origins of Toad-in-the-Hole are a bit murky, though it is generally believed to have originated in Britain—the first recorded recipes date back to the 18th century. The name itself is rather whimsical and does not, as one might imagine, involve actual toads. Toad-in-the-Hole's warming and comforting characteristics make it a lovely option for any festive occasion.

Method

Whisk together the eggs, flour, and milk until a thick batter forms. Oil a 20 cm/8 inch square or round cake tin that fits comfortably in your air fryer, and heat it in the air fryer for 5 minutes at 200C/400F. Pour the batter into the tin while the oil is hot, place the sausages onto the batter, and cook in the air fryer for 15 to 18 minutes or until the batter has risen, is golden and crisp, and the sausages are cooked.

Serves 2 to 4, Preparation time approx 30 mins, Cooking time approx 18 mins

Breaded Scallops

Freshly prepared scallops	450 g	1 lb	2 eggs		
Potato flakes	40 g	1/2 cup	Fine white breadcrumbs	50 g	1/2 cup
Pinch of sea salt and black pepper			Plain/all-purpose flour	15 g	2 tbsp
Spray oil					

About

The reasons for including shellfish in a Christmas feast can vary from family traditions and regional customs to personal preferences for a lighter or more refined meal. In some cultures and coastal regions, shellfish are a staple during the holidays, especially where fresh seafood is abundant. Moreover, shellfish dishes can be versatile and quick to prepare, making them an attractive option for busy holiday cooking schedules.

Method

In a shallow dish, whisk the egg lightly. Combine potato flakes, breadcrumbs, salt, and pepper in a separate dish. Place scallops in a third dish and lightly coat them with flour. Dip each scallop in the whisked egg, then roll it in the potato mixture, pressing lightly so the coating adheres to the scallops.

Lightly spray oil the breaded scallops and cook them in a single layer in the air fryer basket/tray/rack at 190C/370F for 4 minutes or until they turn golden brown. Flip the scallops, give them another spritz of spray oil, and continue cooking for 4 minutes or until the breading becomes firm and crispy.

Serves 4, Preparation time approx 30 mins, Cooking time approx 8 mins

Honey Halibut

Halibut, thick fillets	450 g	1 lb			
Honey marinade					
Salted butter, melted	30 g	1 oz	Ground black pepper		1/2 tsp
Freshly squeezed lemon juice	30 ml	2 tbsp	Honey	15 ml	1 tbsp
Soy sauce		1 tsp	Soy sauce	5 ml	1 tsp
1 garlic clove, grated/shredded			Dried oregano		1/2 tsp
Fresh parsley, finely chopped		1 tbsp	Fresh ginger, peeled, thinly sliced		1 tbsp

About

The tradition of eating halibut or other types of fish during Christmas varies by region and is deeply influenced by cultural, religious, and historical factors. In some families, having halibut for Christmas may be a cherished personal tradition, irrespective of broader cultural or historical reasons. Such traditions often have unique origins and are passed down through generations, adding sentimental value to the holiday meal.

Method

Honey marinade: In a large bowl, blend butter, lemon juice, pepper, honey, soy sauce, garlic, oregano, parsley and ginger to form the honey sauce.

Immerse the halibut in the honey sauce and marinate in the fridge for 30 minutes. Afterwards, remove the fish and discard the leftover sauce. Begin cooking the fish in the air fryer basket/tray/rack at 200C/400F for 3 minutes. Then, lower the temperature to 180C/360F and cook for 5 minutes or until the exterior is golden and cooked.

Serves 2, Preparation time approx 30 mins, Cooking time approx 8 mins

Lobster Tails

1 lime, halved			Sea salt and black pepper to taste		
1 garlic clove, grated/shredded			Zest of half the lime		
Unsalted butter	60 g	2 oz	2 lobster tails, to fit the air fryer basket/tray/rack		

About

Lobster Thermidors' luxurious nature makes it popular for special occasions, including the festive season. The dish is French, created in the late 19th century. It's named after the 11th month in the French Revolutionary calendar, "Thermidor."

Method

Cut the surface of the lobster tails lengthwise and into 1/3 of the meat. Pull apart the cut surface to reveal the meat without tearing the meat. Be careful as the shell can be sharp.

In a saucepan over medium heat, melt the butter with the lime zest and garlic until the garlic becomes aromatic. Place half of the combined mixture into a small bowl and brush it onto the meat of the lobster tails, discarding any leftover brushed butter from the bowl; do not mix it back with the other half still in the saucepan. Season the lobster with salt and pepper.

Cook in the air fryer basket/tray/rack at 190C/370F for 6 minutes or until the lobster meat turns opaque and the internal temperature of the tails reaches 65C/150F. Once cooked, remove from the air fryer, drizzle the remaining melted butter from the saucepan over the lobster meat. Garnish with crushed chilly flakes and slices of chilli or parsley (optional). Cut the remaining half lime into wedges and serve one with each tail.

Serves 2, Preparation time approx 15 mins, Cooking time approx 10 mins

Salmon

Fresh salmon steaks or fillets	450 g	1 lb	Olive oil	30 ml	2 tbsp
Honey	15 ml	1 tbsp	2 garlic cloves, grated/shredded		
Sea salt		1/4 tsp	Ground black pepper		1/2 tsp

About

Salmon is a popular choice for festive occasions in many parts of the world, and its prominence during Christmas is noteworthy. Salmon is often seen as a luxurious food item. It fits right in with the theme of feasting and celebration. It's a dish that stands out and fits in, making it a welcome addition to the Christmas table.

Method

In a small bowl, combine the olive oil, honey, garlic, salt, and pepper. Brush the mixture onto the salmon and refrigerate for 15 minutes. If using fillets, cook the salmon skin side down in the air fryer basket/tray/rack at 200C/400F for 6 to 10 minutes, depending on the thickness, or until the salmon is cooked to your liking and lightly browned.

Consider adding other elements to the air fryer basket, provided space allows. This could include asparagus, leafy greens, green beans, or courgette slices. After cooking, feel free to garnish the salmon with your preferred fresh herbs, a slice of lemon, and perhaps a dash of fresh lemon juice for added zest.

Serves 2, Preparation time approx 15 mins, Cooking time approx 10 mins

Cornish Hens

2 Cornish hens/Cornish game hens			Olive oil		30 ml	2 tbsp
Dried rosemary		1 tsp	Dried thyme			1 tsp
Garlic powder		1/2 tsp	Dried basil			1 tsp
Sea salt		1/2 tsp	Ground black pepper			1/2 tsp

About

Cornish hens, or Cornish game hens, are small, young chickens that are often considered a delicacy suitable for special occasions. Cornish hens have increasingly found their way onto holiday menus. One of the appealing aspects of serving Cornish hens for Christmas is their presentation. Each guest can be served a bird, which feels lavish and eliminates the carving-at-the-table ritual, simplifying the serving process.

Method

Cornish hens/Cornish game hens are small enough to serve whole per guest, halved with sides, or as a shared starter. Depending on their size, you can usually fit two in an air fryer basket, but extra plump birds might require solo cooking.

Combine all the dry ingredients. Coat the hens with olive oil, followed by mixed ingredients and season the hens, ensuring thorough coverage. Cook the hens in the air fryer basket/tray/rack breast-side down at 180C/360F for 20 minutes. Flip the hens and cook for another 20 minutes or until the hens are cooked to your liking. Allow them to rest for 5 minutes before serving. Cranberry sauce is a tasty accompaniment.

Serves 2 to 4, Preparation time approx 30 mins, Cooking time approx 40 mins

Duck Breasts

4 duck breasts, skin on or off			Fresh parsley, finely chopped		1 tbsp
Marinade					
Balsamic vinegar		1 tsp	Dijon mustard	5 ml	1 tsp
2 garlic cloves, grated/shredded			Honey	15 ml	1 tbsp
Sea salt		1/4 tsp	Ground black pepper		1/4 tsp

About

The tradition of serving duck at Christmas can vary by region. Still, it is trendy in certain European countries and among food enthusiasts who appreciate its rich flavour and succulent texture. While turkey is the go-to bird for many during Christmas, only some enjoy its relatively lean and mild meat. Duck offers a more robust and flavourful alternative, especially for smaller gatherings, given its smaller size than a turkey.

Method

Combine the marinade ingredients in a bowl. Score the duck breasts through the skin if the skin is on, and mix them into the marinade. Cover the bowl containing the breasts and marinade, and refrigerate for roughly 2 hours. Remove the breasts from the marinade and dispose of the excess marinade. Cook the breasts in the air fryer basket/tray/rack at 180C/360F for 20 or until cooked to your liking.

Serves 4, Preparation time approx 2 hours, Cooking time approx 20 mins

Sticky Turkey Meatloaf

Minced/ground turkey	700 g	1 1/2 lb	1 egg, beaten		
White breadcrumbs	50 g	1/2 cup	Milk	60 ml	1/4 cup
Garlic powder		1 tsp	Onion powder		1/2 tsp
Sea salt		1/2 tsp	Dijon mustard	15 ml	1 tbsp
Italian seasoning		1 tsp	Tomato ketchup	60 ml	1/2 cup
Sticky sauce					
Tomato Ketchup	60 ml	1/4 cup	Pure maple syrup	45 ml	1 1/2 tbsp

About

The tradition of serving turkey meatloaf during Christmas may not be as widespread as other holiday dishes, but it does offer certain advantages that make it appealing for festive occasions.

Method

Combine all of the ingredients, but not the sticky sauce ingredients and the turkey, in a large bowl. Mix the ingredients by hand or utensils, then mix in the turkey. Shape the mixture into a deep 18 cm/7-inch baking/roasting tin.

Cook in the air fryer at 180C/360F for 20 minutes. Meanwhile, prepare the sauce and after the 20 minutes, glaze the meatloaf. Cover the meatloaf loosely with foil and cook another 10 minutes.

Check internal temperature. If it's 70C/170F, keep covered and rest for 10 minutes before serving. If below, cook another 5 minutes without the foil until it reaches the desired internal temperature.

Serves 4, Preparation time approx 30 mins, Cooking time approx 10 mins

Stuffed Chicken & Bacon

4 chicken breasts, boneless, skinless			4 bacon rashers/slices	
Cheddar cheese, grated/shredded	60 g	1/2 cup	Fresh parsley, finely chopped	2 tbsp
Chives, chopped		1 tbsp	Ground black pepper	1/4 tsp
Toothpicks or cocktail sticks			Spray oil	

About

Stuffed chicken and bacon is a delightful culinary twist on traditional festive recipes. Combining the rich flavours of chicken and bacon with savoury stuffing makes it a popular choice for those looking to diversify their Christmas dinner menu.

Method

Cut a deep pocket in the thickest part of each chicken breast. Mix cheese, parsley, chives, and pepper in a small bowl. Stuff the mixture into the chicken breast pockets. Wrap each breast with bacon, securing it with toothpicks or cocktail sticks if needed.

Spray the chicken with oil and cook them in the air fryer basket/tray/rack at 200C/400F for 15 to 20 minutes for an internal temperature of 75C/170F.

Serves 4, Preparation time approx 40 mins, Cooking time approx 20 mins

Turkey Croquettes

Spray oil			Panko or coarse breadcrumbs	150 g	1 1/2 cups
Pre-made mashed potatoes	450 g	2 cups	Parmesan cheese, grated/shredded	50 g	1/2 cup
1 small onion, peeled, finely chopped			Swiss cheese, grated/shredded	60 g	1/2 cup
Fresh rosemary, finely chopped		1 tbsp	Dried sage		1/2 tsp
Sea salt		1/2 tsp	Ground black pepper		1/2 tsp
2 eggs, beaten			Finely chopped cooked turkey	300 g	2 1/2 cups

About

Turkey croquettes can make a delightful addition to Christmas festivities or offer a creative way to repurpose leftover turkey from your holiday feast. This dish embodies the spirit of culinary innovation and holiday tradition, effectively merging the two.

Method

Mix mashed potatoes, cheese, shallot, sage, rosemary, salt and pepper in a large bowl. Add the turkey and form the mixture into 10 burgers/patties. Whisk the eggs and water in one bowl and place the breadcrumbs in another. Dip the burgers/patties in the egg, then coat with the breadcrumbs.

Lightly spray oil the burgers/patties, now croquettes, and cook them in a single layer in the air fryer basket/tray/rack at 180C/360F for 8 minutes or until golden brown and crispy. Flip them halfway.

Serves 4, Preparation time approx 30 mins, Cooking time approx 8 mins

Turkey Crown

1 turkey crown, thawed	1.4 kg	3 lb	6 rashers/slices of streaky bacon		
Sea salt		1/2 tsp	Ground black pepper		1/2 tsp
Dried thyme		1/2 tsp	Dried rosemary		1/2 tsp
Garlic powder		1/2 tsp	Olive oil	15 ml	1 tbsp

About

For several reasons, serving a turkey crown at Christmas has become an increasingly popular choice. A turkey crown, the breast meat on the bone, is easier and quicker to cook than a whole turkey. It takes up less oven space than a whole turkey, leaving room for all the other delicious sides and trimmings that often accompany a Christmas meal.

Method

Remove the thawed or fresh turkey crown from the packaging and pat dry with paper towels. Brush with the olive oil and season with salt, pepper, thyme, rosemary, and garlic powder. Lay bacon rashers over the crown and secure it with toothpicks if needed.

Cook at 180C/360F in the air fryer basket/tray/rack for 30 minutes, leaving enough space for air circulation. Use a meat thermometer to check the turkey's internal temperature; it should reach 74C/165F in the thickest part. If needed, continue cooking, checking every 5 minutes until the required internal temperature is reached. Once fully cooked, rest the turkey crown for 10 minutes before serving.

Serves 4 to 6, Preparation time approx 15 mins, Cooking time approx 30 mins

Turkey Steaks

4 thick turkey breast steaks		Sea salt	1/2 tsp
Ground black pepper	1/4 tsp	Spray oil	
Italian seasoning	1/2 tsp	Smoked paprika	1/2 tsp
Garlic powder	1/2 tsp	Onion powder	1/2 tsp

About

The turkey is native to North America. When European explorers like the Spanish and later the English came to the New World in the 16th century, they encountered this bird and began to export it back to Europe. While goose and peacock had been the preferred choices for festive meals in medieval England, it's believed that King Henry VIII was the first English monarch to have turkey for Christmas in the 16th century.

Method

Combine the ingredients in a bowl, other than the turkey and oil, then season the turkey steaks with the mixture on both sides. Spray the steaks with oil and cook them in the air fryer basket/tray/rack at 200C/400F for 8 minutes or until golden, turning them over midway. The cooking time might vary based on the turkey's thickness, but ensure the internal temperature reaches 75C/170F at the thickest part.

Serves 4, Preparation time approx 20 mins, Cooking time approx 8 mins

Whole Chicken

1 whole chicken, thawed			Olive oil	30 ml	2 tbsp
Garlic powder		1 tsp	Paprika		1 tsp
Sea salt		1/2 tsp	Ground black pepper		1 tsp

About

Chicken is different from the traditional centrepiece of a Christmas dinner; that role is more commonly filled by turkey, goose, or sometimes beef or ham. However, chicken has found its way into many Christmas feasts. Chicken is generally less expensive than other meats. A chicken is smaller and easier to manage, and a small chicken can fit most air fryer baskets. Some people prefer the leaner meat of chicken over the more robust flavours of turkey or goose. Chicken is a versatile and practical option that can find a place at the Christmas table.

Method

Combine the olive oil, salt, garlic powder, paprika, and black pepper in a bowl, and rub or brush the mixture over the chicken. Leave it to stand for 15 minutes in a cool place.

Cook it in the air fryer basket/tray/rack, breast side up, at 180C/360F for 30 to 40 minutes or until the internal temperature of the chicken, tested deep into the thigh or breast, reaches 74C/165F. Flip the chicken to breast side down halfway through cooking.

Serves 4, Preparation time approx 30 mins, Cooking time approx 40 mins

Whole Pheasant

Sea salt		1/4 tsp	Ground black pepper		1/4 tsp
Olive oil	15 ml	1 tbsp	Garlic powder		1 tsp
Paprika		1 tsp	Italian seasoning		1 tsp

1 whole pheasant, thawed or fresh. If air fryer space is limited, consider halving the pheasant and reducing the cooking time by 10 minutes

Brine can be used for other game birds and turkey

Water	2 l	4 pints	Sea salt	20 g	2 tbsp
Brown sugar	50 g	1/4 cup	Honey	60 ml	1/4 cup
1 onion, peeled, finely chopped			4 garlic cloves, finely chopped		
1 celery stalk, finely chopped			Lemon juice	60 ml	1/4 cup

About

The tradition of serving game birds during festive occasions has a long and storied history, particularly in Europe. Pheasant, specifically, has been a popular choice for Christmas feasts and other special occasions for several centuries.

Method

Brining: Heat water in a saucepan until steaming. Add salt, brown sugar, and honey, then stir until dissolved. Let it cool to room temperature. Mix in onion, garlic, celery, and lemon. Add the pheasant, cover, and refrigerate for at least 12 hours or overnight.

Pheasant: Remove the pheasant from the brine, pat it dry with kitchen roll/towel and remove water from the cavity. Once dry, rub the olive oil all over it. Combine the other ingredients in a bowl and coat the pheasant with it. Cook in the air fryer basket/tray/rack for up to 40 minutes or until it reaches an internal temperature of 75C/170F. Remove the pheasant and leave it to stand for 15 minutes before slicing.

Serves 4, Preparation time approx 12 hours, Cooking time approx 40 mins

Brussels Sprouts & Chestnuts

Brussels sprouts	450 g	1 lb	Olive oil	15 ml	1 tbsp
Garlic powder		1/2 tsp	Sea salt		1/2 tsp
Ground black pepper		1/4 tsp	Chestnuts, ready to eat	180 g	6 oz
2 rashers/slices of bacon, finely chopped (optional)					

About

The tradition of serving Brussels sprouts at Christmas is particularly strong in the United Kingdom and other countries influenced by British culinary customs. These tiny cabbages have been a staple of the festive table for many generations, but their association with Christmas is fascinating in its own right. Brussels sprouts are believed to have been cultivated in Belgium—specifically in the Brussels region—since the 16th century, which is how they got their name. However, their ancestry can be traced back to ancient Roman times.

Method

Remove any dead or discoloured leaves. Halve any larger Brussels sprouts, leave smaller ones whole and place them in a large bowl. Halve the chestnuts and add them to the bowl containing the sprouts. Add the chopped bacon (optional). Drizzle the sprouts, chestnuts, and bacon with olive oil and toss well.

Sprinkle with garlic powder, salt, and black pepper, and toss again. Cook in the air fryer basket/tray/rack at 190C/370F for 16 minutes or until fork tender, shaking the basket/tray/rack halfway through.

Serves 4 to 6, Preparation time approx 15 mins, Cooking time approx 16 mins

Cauliflower Cheese

1 head of cauliflower cut into florets			Butter	30 g	1 oz
Plain/all-purpose flour	30 g	1/4 cup	Dijon mustard	5 ml	1 tsp
Garlic powder		1/4 tsp	Milk	250 ml	1 cup
Ground nutmeg		1/4 tsp	Pinch of sea salt and black pepper		
Cheddar cheese, grated/shredded	120 g	1 cup	Parmesan, grated/shredded	25 g	1/4 cup
Extra mature cheddar, grated/shredded	30 g	1/4 cup			

About

The tradition of incorporating vegetable dishes into Christmas feasts is longstanding, and cauliflower cheese serves as a creamy, comforting side that pairs well with various main courses commonly served during the holiday, such as roast beef, turkey, or ham.

Method

Boil the cauliflower florets in salted water for 5 minutes. Drain and set aside. In a saucepan, melt butter and stir in flour, cooking for a minute. Add salt, pepper, mustard, garlic, and nutmeg. Gradually whisk in the milk until smooth, then remove from heat. Mix in cheddar cheese, stirring until melted. If needed, briefly return to heat.

Combine the florets with the cheese sauce. Transfer this mixture to an air fryer-friendly dish and top with extra mature cheddar, then top that with the Parmesan. Cook in the air fryer at 200C/400F for 8 minutes, checking on it until the cheese has melted and is golden brown and dark brown in places.

Serves 4, Preparation time approx 30 mins, Cooking time approx 12 mins

Dinner Rolls

Unsalted butter, room temperature	60 g	2 oz	Sea salt			1/2 tsp
Milk	60 ml	1/4 cup	Bread flour	240 g		2 cups
Granulated sugar	30 g	3 tbsp	Active dry yeast			2 tsp
Warm water	60 ml	1/4 cup				

About

Today's dinner rolls are a product of centuries of baking evolution. They can range from simple to gourmet, with herbs, cheeses, and grains. They have become a staple in many cultures, mainly Western dining settings, especially during holidays and gatherings.

Method

Mix water, yeast, and 1 tsp of the granulated sugar in a jug and let it stand for 10 minutes. In a bowl, combine the flour, remaining sugar, and salt. Add the yeast mixture, milk, and butter, then mix well. Knead the dough on a floured surface for 10 minutes or use a stand mixer. Place the dough in a greased bowl, cover it, and let it rise for 1 hour.

Segment the risen dough into 12 rolls and place them in a parchment paper lined air fryer basket or a tray in an air fryer tray or rack. Ensure the dough balls are close together but not quite touching. Allow them to rise again in the lined air fryer basket or a tray for 30 minutes. This should allow the balls to rise slightly and touch each other.

There's no need to preheat the air fryer. Place the basket or tray in the air fryer and cook at 150C/300F for 15 minutes or until golden. Brush with melted butter and sprinkle with coarse sea salt (optional)

Serves 6, Preparation time approx 1 hour, Cooking time approx 15 mins

Garlic Butter Mushrooms

Small mushrooms or larger cut in half	450 g	1 lb	Olive oil	15 ml	1 tbsp
Soy sauce	30 ml	2 tbsp	Ground black pepper		1/4 tsp
2 garlic cloves peeled, grated/shredded			10 chives or 2 spring onions, chopped		
Butter	30 g	1 oz			

About

Garlic butter mushrooms are a popular side dish often enjoyed during Christmas festivities. Combining earthy mushrooms with the rich, aromatic flavours of garlic and butter makes for a delicious accompaniment that pairs well with various traditional Christmas mains, such as roast turkey, beef, or lamb.

Method

Combine the olive oil, soy sauce, and pepper in a bowl and mix well with the mushrooms. Cook the mushrooms in the air fryer basket/tray/rack at 200C/400F for 6 minutes, giving the basket a shake halfway through. Once cooked, transfer the mushrooms to a bowl. Melt the butter with the garlic in a small saucepan, pour the mixture on the mushrooms, garnish with the chives or spring onions and serve.

Serves 4, Preparation time approx 15 mins, Cooking time approx 6 mins

Green Bean Casserole

Crispy fried onions	120 g	2 cups	Mature cheddar, grated/shredded	60 g	1/2 cup
4 garlic cloves, grated/shredded		1 tsp	Sea salt		1/2 tsp
Ground black pepper		1/4 tsp	Cooked green beans	600 g	4 cups
Milk	125 g	1/2 cup	Parmesan cheese, grated/shredded	25 g	1/4 cup
1 tin/can of cream of mushroom soup					

About

Green bean casserole is a popular side dish often served during Christmas feasts. Its deliciousness and simplicity make it an appealing option for Christmas globally.

Method

Combine the cream of mushroom soup, milk, green beans, salt, pepper, garlic, cheese, and 60 g/1 cup of the fried onions in a large bowl, then into an ovenproof casserole dish. Ensure the dish fits comfortably within your air fryer basket/tray/rack.

No need to preheat. Place the dish inside the air fryer and cook at 160C/120F for 25 minutes. After this time, Stir the green bean mixture well.

Scatter the remaining fried onions over the top and cook at the same temperature for up to 5 minutes without burning the mixture or onions.

Serves 4 to 6, Preparation time approx 20 mins, Cooking time approx 30 mins

Hasselback Potatoes

4 floury potatoes such as Maris Piper or King Edwards or Idaho			
Olive oil	15 ml	1 tbsp	2 rashers/slices of uncooked bacon (optional)
Sea salt		1/2 tsp	1 onion, peeled, sliced
Ground black pepper		1/2 tsp	

About

Originally from Sweden, Hasselback potatoes have found their way into Christmas meals in various parts of the world and are named after the Hasselbacken Hotel in Stockholm, where they were first served. One of the most striking features of Hasselback potatoes is their visual presentation. The fanned-out slices create an appealing aesthetic that can elevate the overall look of a holiday meal. This makes them popular for occasions where presentation matters, like Christmas.

Method

Slice the potatoes thinly without cutting through the base. Situate the potatoes in a bowl and brush over them with olive oil. If desired, insert small bacon pieces with the onion into the slits for extra flavour while ensuring the air fryer can heat the potatoes thoroughly. Season with salt and pepper and cook the potatoes in the air fryer basket/tray/rack at 180C/360F for 15 minutes or until crispy and cooked.

Serves 4, Preparation time approx 30 mins, Cooking time approx 20 mins

Marmite or Vegemite Roast Potatoes

4 medium-sized potatoes, skin on or off			Olive oil	30 ml	2 tbsp
Marmite or vegemite	10 ml	2 tsp	Sea salt		1/4 tsp
Ground black pepper		1/4 tsp	Freshly chopped herbs of choice		2 tsp

About

Marmite or Vegemite in roast potatoes brings a unique blend of slightly salty yet strong flavours. Whether served as part of a Sunday roast or gracing the Christmas dinner table, Marmite or Vegemite roast potatoes are a modern classic. The practical aspect of using Marmite or Vegemite as a coating helps to achieve a delightful, crispy exterior, thus solving one of the age-old challenges of roast potato preparation.

Method

Slice the potatoes (if they are starchy, soak the chunks for 30 minutes before drying them). Thoroughly mix the oil, Marmite or Vegemite, herbs, salt, and pepper in a large bowl. This might take a little time, as the Marmite or Vegemite can be thick. It is possible to slightly warm the Marmite or Vegemite so that it mixes more easily. Once mixed well, add the potato and ensure an even coating. Cover and leave to stand for 30 minutes.

After 30 minutes, stir the potatoes in the mixture again, then cook in the air fryer basket/tray/rack at 200C/400F for 20 minutes or until crispy and golden and soft on the inside. Shake the basket halfway through cooking.

Serves 4 to 6, Preparation time approx 1 hour, Cooking time approx 20 mins

Mashed Potatoes

Small potatoes, not baby potatoes	900 g	2 lb	Olive oil	30 ml	2 tbsp
Unsalted butter	60 g	1/4 cup	Heavy cream, or double cream	60 ml	1/4 cup
Garlic powder		1/2 tsp	Sea salt		1/2 tsp
Ground black pepper		1/4 tsp			

About

The serving of mashed potatoes at Christmas dinners has diverse historical origins. Potatoes became a staple food in European diets after they were introduced from the Americas in the late 16th century. They were relatively easy to grow and store, making them a reliable food source.

Method

Place the potatoes (skin on) in a bowl and season them with the oil, salt, pepper, and garlic powder, ensuring they are well-coated, and wrap each potato in foil.

Cook in the air fryer basket/tray/rack for 25 minutes, then test the potatoes for tenderness with a fork. If they still need to be tender, cook for 5 minutes or until they are fork-tender. Once cooked, cut the potatoes in half and squeeze the flesh into a bowl (you can also cut up the skins and add those after mashing the flesh if you wish); add butter and cream, and mash until smooth.

Serves 4 to 6, Preparation time approx 20 mins, Cooking time approx 25 mins

Mixed Roasted Vegetables

1 yellow bell pepper, deseeded, chopped			2 onions, peeled, chopped		
1 red bell pepper, deseeded, chopped			1 head of broccoli, cut into florets		
1 courgette/zucchini, chopped			Mushrooms, chopped or halved	225 g	8 oz
Dried parsley		1/4 tsp	Sea salt		1/4 tsp
Ground black pepper		1/4 tsp	Italian seasoning		1/4 tsp
Olive oil	15 ml	1 tbsp			

About

The tradition of serving roasted vegetables during Christmas feasts has evolved over centuries, shaped by agricultural practices, religious customs, and culinary trends. Historically, the types of food that were available for these celebrations were those that were in season or could be stored for long periods.

Method

Combine all ingredients in a large bowl, ensuring every item gets an even coverage. Cook in the air fryer basket/tray/rack. Depending on your device's capacity, you may need to cook in multiple batches and cook at 200C/400F for 15 minutes or until tender.

Serves 4, Preparation time approx 30 mins, Cooking time approx 15 mins

Pork Stuffing Balls

Minced/ground pork	700 g	1 1/2 lb	White breadcrumbs	100 g	1 cup
Milk	125 ml	1/2 cup	2 eggs, beaten		
2 celery stalks, finely chopped			1 onion, peeled, finely chopped		
Fresh sage, finely chopped		1 tbsp	Fresh rosemary, finely chopped		1 tbsp
Dried thyme		1/2 tsp	Fresh parsley, finely chopped		1 tbsp
Sea salt		1/2 tsp	Ground black pepper		1/4 tsp

About

Stuffing, traditionally used to fill the cavity of poultry before roasting, dates back centuries. Pork stuffing balls are essentially compact versions of traditional stuffing. They're made by combining minced pork with a variety of ingredients.

Method

Mix the milk and bread crumbs in a small bowl and set aside. In a larger bowl, combine all the ingredients, including the breadcrumb mixture, using your hands until evenly mixed. Shape this mixture into balls, using roughly 2 tbsp for each.

Cook the stuffing balls in the air fryer basket/tray/rack for 10 minutes, turning them over halfway through. Ensure they're cooked until golden brown with an internal temperature of 70C/160F. Serve warm or cold.

Serves 4 to 6, Preparation time approx 30 mins, Cooking time approx 10 mins

Potato Gratin

Soft cheese of choice: Gruyere, Gouda, Swiss, Cheddar, Mozzarella, grated/shredded				240 g	2 cups
Heavy cream, or double cream	180 ml	3/4 cup	Potatoes	900 g	2 lb
2 garlic cloves, grated/shredded			Pinch of salt and pepper		

About

Potato gratin, or Dauphinoise potatoes, is a popular side dish often served during Christmas celebrations. This classic French dish is characterised by its luxurious layers of thinly sliced potatoes, rich cream, and often a generous helping of cheese.

Method

Peel the potatoes and slice them into 6 mm / 1/4-inch thick pieces. In a saucepan, parboil for 5 minutes. Drain the water and set the slices aside to cool. Combine the garlic and cream in a bowl.

In a baking/roasting tin or ovenproof dish which fits comfortably in the air fryer, arrange a layer of potato slices. Pour a third of the cream mixture over the potatoes, followed by a sprinkling of grated/shredded cheese. Season lightly with a bit of salt and pepper. Repeat these layers twice more, finishing with cream mixture and cheese.

Cover the tin with foil and cook the potato gratin in the air fryer at 170C/340F for 30 minutes or until the potato slices are fork tender. Next, remove the foil and cook at 200C/400F for 10 minutes or until the top is golden brown and bubbling. Remove from the air fryer and allow to rest for 5 minutes before serving.

Serves 4 to 6, Preparation time approx 40 mins, Cooking time approx 40 mins

Potato Salad

10 chives or 2 spring onions, chopped			Freshly squeezed lemon juice	15 ml	1 tbsp
Sour/soured cream	125 ml	1/2 cup	5 bacon rashers/slices		
Potatoes, peeled, diced	900 g	2 lb	1 packet of dry French onion soup		
Mayonnaise	250 ml	1 cup	Olive oil	30 ml	2 tbsp

About

Potato salad is a dish that spans cultures and continents. Its presence during Christmas celebrations. One of the earliest forms of potato salad originates from Germany. As German immigrants moved to other parts of the world, they brought their culinary traditions, including the potato salad.

Method

Mix the oil, 60 ml / 1/4 cup of mayonnaise, and the dry soup in a bowl. Add the potatoes and ensure they're well coated with the mixture. Remove the potatoes from the mixture and cook them in the air fryer basket/tray/rack at 200C/400F for 10 minutes.

Give the basket a shake to move the potatoes around, and lay the bacon rashers/slices over the potatoes. Adjust the temperature to 160C/320F and cook for 10 minutes or until the bacon is cooked and the potatoes are tender.

Blend the remaining mayonnaise, sour/soured cream, lemon juice, and chives or spring onions. Once the bacon and potatoes are cooked, place the potatoes in a serving dish and pour over the sour/soured cream blend. Roughly chop the bacon and sprinkle over the potato salad before serving hot or cold.

Serves 4 to 6, Preparation time approx 30 mins, Cooking time approx 20 mins

Roast Potatoes

4 large potatoes, peeled, cut into 4 cm/1 1/2 inch chunks (if the potatoes are starchy, soak the chunks for 30 minutes before drying them					
Olive oil	30 ml	2 tbsp	Garlic powder		1/2 tsp
Onion powder		1/2 tsp	Dried thyme		1/2 tsp
Dried oregano		1/2 tsp	Smoked paprika		1/2 tsp
Sea salt		1/2 tsp	Ground black pepper		1/2 tsp

About

Roast potatoes in Christmas feasts likely evolved naturally from their popularity in Sunday roasts. Roast potatoes have become a festive staple through cultural habits and gastronomic satisfaction. Their presence enriches the table and pays homage to centuries of culinary history.

Method

Mix all ingredients, including the potato chunks, in a large bowl until evenly coated and leave them to stand for 15 minutes. Cook the potatoes in a single layer in the air fryer basket/tray/rack at 200C/400F for 15 minutes or until the chunks are fork-tender with a crisp exterior. Shake the basket halfway through cooking so they are evenly cooked.

Serves 4 to 6, Preparation time approx 30 mins, Cooking time approx 15 mins

Stuffed Mushrooms

4 Portobello mushrooms		Cheddar cheese, grated/shredded	60 g	1/2 cup
2 garlic cloves, grated/shredded		Freshly chopped herbs of choice		2 tbsp
2 cooked rashers/slices of bacon (optional)		Ground black pepper		1/4 tsp
1 onion, peeled, finely chopped		Spray oil		

About

Stuffed mushrooms offer an interesting departure from more conventional Christmas fare, yet they could be an excellent addition to a festive meal. They cater well to vegetarian guests, offering a hearty and flavourful option that can easily be adapted to suit vegan diets. They can be prepared in advance and quickly cooked or reheated, providing a fuss-free yet elegant option that doesn't require last-minute preparations.

Method

Combine the cheese, onion, garlic, pepper, optional bacon, and herbs in a bowl and set aside. Clean the mushrooms, removing stems and hollowing out the gills. Lightly spray oil the mushrooms and cook them in the air fry basket/tray/rack at 200C/400F for 8 minutes. Then, fill each mushroom with the cheese mixture and cook for another 5 minutes or until the cheese has melted and the mushrooms are done.

Serves 4, Preparation time approx 30 mins, Cooking time approx 8 mins

Stuffing Balls

Spray oil			Chicken broth or stock	60 ml	1/4 cup
1 egg, beaten			Ground black pepper		1/4 tsp
Sea salt		1/2 tsp	Chicken or other poultry seasoning		1/2 tsp
Dried parsley		1 tsp	Stale white bread, cubed	400 g	6 cups
2 celery sticks, finely chopped			1 onion, peeled, finely chopped		
Butter, room temperature	30 g	1 oz			

About

The tradition of preparing stuffing—or "dressing," as it's known in some regions—for Christmas or other festive occasions has a long history that dates back centuries. The stuffing ball, a portion shaped into a small round form and often baked separately from the main dish, has become popular as a convenient way to serve stuffing in individual pieces.

Method

In a small saucepan over medium heat, melt the butter and sauté the celery and onion until they soften, which should take around 5 minutes.

Combine the bread, parsley, poultry seasoning, salt, and pepper in a bowl. Add the sautéed onion and celery. Gradually mix in the egg, followed by the chicken stock, until well combined. Shape into golf-ball-sized stuffing balls and chill for at least 15 minutes.

Lightly spray oil the balls and cook them in the air fryer basket/tray/rack, ensuring they don't touch, at 180C/360F for 5 minutes. Turn them over and continue cooking for another 3 minutes or until they are golden brown and crispy on the outside.

Serves 4 to 6, Preparation time approx 30 mins, Cooking time approx 8 mins

Traditional Stuffing

Butter	60 g	2 oz	Olive oil	30 ml	2 tbsp
2 large onions, peeled, diced			2 celery stalks/sticks, chopped		
3 garlic cloves, grated/shredded			Day-old white bread, cubed or crumbled	300 g	4 cups
Dried thyme		1/2 tsp	Dried rosemary		1/2 tsp
Ground sage		1/2 tsp	Chicken broth or stock	60 ml	1/4 cup
Sea salt		1/4 tsp	Ground black pepper		1/4 tsp

About

Stuffing, or dressing as it is known in some parts, is a beloved component of Christmas meals across various cultures. The basic concept—bread or grains mixed with other ingredients and seasonings—transcends geographical boundaries, but the specific ingredients and preparation methods can differ from place to place.

Method

Melt the butter with the olive oil over medium-high heat in a large frying pan/skillet. Add the onions, celery, and garlic, and cook until softened and fragrant, about 5 minutes.

Transfer the sautéed vegetables to a large bowl, then add the bread, thyme, rosemary, sage, chicken stock, salt, and pepper. Mix well. Cook the stuffing in an oven-proof dish in the air fryer at 180C/360F for roughly 15 minutes or until the top is lightly golden brown and any liquid has gone into the mixture. Fluff it as best you can and leave it to rest.

Serves 4 to 6, Preparation time approx 30 mins, Cooking time approx 15 mins

Yorkshire Puddings

2 large eggs, beaten			Milk	170 ml	3/4 cup
Plain/all-purpose flour	90 g	3/4 cup	Extra virgin olive oil	30 ml	2 tbsp
Sea salt		1/2 tsp			

About

While their original culinary partnership was with roast beef, these puffed-up delicacies have increasingly found a place at the Christmas dinner table. They are adored by many and offer an additional textural experience to the meal. The inclusion of Yorkshire puddings adds a touch of indulgence.

Method

Add eggs, milk, flour, and salt to create a thick batter, then thoroughly oil 8 individual Yorkshire pudding moulds or muffin tins. Depending on your air fryer's size, you might need to work in batches. Start the air fryer to 200C/400F or 220C/430F if it goes that high, with the oiled moulds inside, and heat them for 6 minutes.

Once heated, swiftly fill each mould halfway with batter, straight onto the little pool of oil now settled at the bottom of each mould. Cook for 10 minutes or until the puddings are golden, crispy, and inflated. You may not have to cook as long with higher heat.

Serves 4, Preparation time approx 30 mins, Cooking time approx 10 mins

Cabbage

1 head of green cabbage, cored, sliced		Olive oil	15 ml	1 tbsp
Ground ginger	1/2 tsp	Pinch of sea salt and black pepper		

Method

Discard the core from the sliced cabbage and transfer the cabbage to a bowl. Toss it with olive oil, ground ginger, salt, and pepper. If desired, include bacon or onion strips. Cook the cabbage in the air fryer basket/tray/rack at 190C/370F for 8 to 10 minutes, stirring occasionally.

Serves 4 to 6, Preparation time approx 20 mins, Cooking time approx 10 mins

Crispy Cauliflower

Ground black pepper	1/4 tsp	Sea salt	1/2 tsp
Ground turmeric	1/2 tsp	Smoked paprika	1/2 tsp
Olive oil	15 ml 1 tbsp	1 head of cauliflower, cut into florets	

Method

Combine the ingredients, other than the florets, in a large bowl and mix well. Add the florets and stir them in the mixture until thoroughly coated. Cook them in the air fryer basket/tray/rack at 200C/400F for 15 minutes or until cooked to your liking; flip them from time to time for even cooking.

Serves 4, Preparation time approx 30 mins, Cooking time approx 15 mins

Crispy Red Cabbage

1 red cabbage, loose leaves removed, cut into quarters or as many slices as there are guests					
Spray oil			Sea salt		1/2 tsp
Garlic powder		1/2 tsp	Onion powder		1/2 tsp

Method

Spray the cabbage slices with oil and season them with salt, garlic and onion powder while doing your best to keep the slices from falling apart. Cook them seasoned in the air fryer basket/tray/rack at 200C/400F for 10 minutes or until crisp yet tender.

Serves 4 to 6, Preparation time approx 30 mins, Cooking time approx 15 mins

Fried Green Beans

Fresh green beans	450 g	1 lb	Olive oil	15 ml	1 tbsp
Sea salt		1/2 tsp	Ground black pepper		1/2 tsp

Method

Trim and halve green beans for uniform size. Toss with olive oil, salt, and pepper in a large bowl. Cook them in a single layer in the air fryer basket/tray/rack; cook in batches, if necessary, at 190C/370F for 8 minutes or until crispy and tender. Garnish and serve.

Serves 4 to 6, Preparation time approx 10 mins, Cooking time approx 8 mins

Fried Leeks

2 leeks, sliced across to create circles or lengthways to create strings, removing the dark green leaves or parts					
Spray oil			Olive oil	15 ml	1 tbsp
Dried thyme		1/4 tsp	Sea salt		1/4 tsp

Method

Mix the leeks with olive oil, thyme, and salt in a bowl and cook them in the basket/tray/rack at 200C/400F for 8 minutes while stirring occasionally. Remove when done to your liking.

Serves 4 to 6, Preparation time approx 30 mins, Cooking time approx 15 mins

Fried Onions

| 2 onions, peeled, sliced | | | Olive oil | 15 ml | 1 tbsp |
| Sea salt | | 1/2 tsp | | | |

Method

Combine the sliced onions with olive oil and salt, ensuring they are evenly coated. Cook in the air fryer basket/tray/rack at 200C/400F for 5 minutes, giving them a shake midway, until the onions are cooked to your liking.

Serves 4 to 6, Preparation time approx 30 mins, Cooking time approx 15 mins

Garlic Broccoli

Broccoli florets	450 g	1 lb	Olive oil	30 ml	2 tbsp
4 garlic cloves, grated/shredded			1 small onion, grated/shredded		
Pinch of sea salt and black pepper			Parmesan cheese, grated/shredded	30 g	1 oz

Method

Combine the ingredients, other than the florets, in a large bowl and mix well. Add the florets and stir them in the mixture until thoroughly coated. Cook them in the air fryer basket/tray/rack at 200C/400F for 6 minutes or until cooked to your liking.

Serves 4, Preparation time approx 20 mins, Cooking time approx 6 mins

Honey Parsnips

Pinch of sea salt and black pepper			Olive oil	15 ml	1 tbsp
4 parsnips, peeled, cut into thick sticks			Honey	15 ml	1 tbsp

Method

In a bowl, combine the parsnips with oil, honey, salt, and pepper, ensuring they are well-coated. Cook the seasoned parsnips in the air fryer basket/tray/rack at 200C/400F for 15 minutes, stirring occasionally and until they turn golden.

Serves 4 to 6, Preparation time approx 20 mins, Cooking time approx 15 mins

Red Roast Potatoes

Red potatoes, skin on, cut into chunks	900 g	2 lb	Olive oil	30 ml	2 tbsp
Dried rosemary		1 tsp	2 garlic cloves, grated/shredded		
Sea salt		1 tsp	Ground black pepper		1/2 tsp

Method

Combine the oil, garlic, rosemary, salt, and pepper in a large bowl. Add the potato chunks and toss them in the mixture until thoroughly coated. Cook them in the air fryer basket/tray/rack at 200C/400F for 15 minutes or until they turn golden and are cooked.

Serves 4 to 6, Preparation time approx 20 mins, Cooking time approx 15 mins

Roasted Tinned/Canned Potatoes

Enough tinned/canned potatoes for the number of people you plan to serve					
Olive oil			15 ml	1 tbsp	Pinch of sea salt and black pepper

Method

Drain and pat dry the tinned/canned potatoes—any particularly large ones, cut in half. Toss them with olive oil, salt, and pepper in a bowl. Cook them in the air fryer basket/tray/rack at 190C/370F for 20 minutes or until golden and have a crust on the surface, shaking the potatoes halfway.

Preparation time approx 20 mins, Cooking time approx 20 mins

Sweet Potato Chunks

Sweet potatoes, peeled, cubed	700 g	1 1/2 lb	Olive oil	15 ml	1 tbsp
Ground black pepper		1/4 tsp	Coarse sea salt		1/2 tsp

Method

Place the sweet potatoes in a bowl with the oil, salt and pepper. Toss the chunks to ensure all of the pieces are evenly coated. Cook them in a single in the air fryer basket/tray/rack, cooking in batches if necessary, for 10 minutes. Shake them halfway.

Serves 4 to 6, Preparation time approx 20 mins, Cooking time approx 10 mins

Savoury Carrots

Fresh parsley, finely chopped		1 tbsp	Sea salt		1/2 tsp
Olive oil	15 ml	1 tbsp	Ground black pepper		1/4 tsp
Garlic powder		1/2 tsp	Paprika		1/2 tsp
Carrots, peeled and sliced lengthways if large, or use small or baby carrots				450 g	1 lb

Method

Toss carrots in olive oil, garlic powder, paprika and salt and pepper in a large bowl. Cook in the air fryer basket/tray/rack at 190C/370F for 15 minutes. Garnish with parsley.

Serves 4 to 6, Preparation time approx 10 mins, Cooking time approx 15 mins

Traditional Roasted Chestnuts

| Chestnuts | 450 g | 1 lb | Pinch of salt and pepper to taste | | |

Method

Boil a pan of water and set aside. Wash and dry chestnuts in cold water, then score a cross on the top surface of each, cutting down through the skin and brown layer. Soak them in the hot water for 5 minutes. Remove them from the water, then cook them in the air fryer basket/tray/rack at 200C/400F for up to 15 minutes, depending on the size. They are cooked when the skin partly peels back, revealing the flesh. Allow them to cool slightly so that you can enjoy peeling and eating them. Add salt and pepper to taste.

Serves 4 to 6, Preparation time approx 20 mins, Cooking time approx 15 mins

Turnip Fries/Chips

Sea salt		1/2 tsp	Ground cumin		1/2 tsp
Onion powder		1/4 tsp	Paprika		1/4 tsp
Garlic powder		1/4 tsp	Olive oil	15 ml	1 tbsp
2 turnips, peeled, cut into fries/chips			Ground black pepper		1/4 tsp

Method

In a large bowl, combine the ingredients, other than the turnips, and mix well. Add the turnip fries/chips and toss them in the mixture until evenly coated. Cook them in a single layer in the air fryer basket at 190C/370F for 15 minutes or until golden and crisp. Shake the basket/tray/rack halfway through.

Serves 4 to 6, Preparation time approx 30 mins, Cooking time approx 15 mins

Apple Crumble

Tarty and firm apples, peeled, sliced	450 g	1 lb	Granulated sugar	50 g	1/4 cup
Freshly squeezed lemon juice	5 ml	1 tsp	Ground cinnamon		1/4 tsp
Sea salt		1/4 tsp	Ground nutmeg		1/4 tsp
Plain/all-purpose flour	60 g	1/2 cup	Brown sugar	50 g	1/4 cup
Rolled oats	60 g	1/2 cup	Unsalted butter, cold and cubed	120 g	4 oz

About

While apple crumble is less traditional at Christmas than mince pies or Christmas pudding is, it is not out of place on a Christmas dinner table. The warm, spiced apple filling and buttery crumb topping can undoubtedly evoke a sense of festive comfort and joy. Its versatility and universally pleasing nature make it an excellent choice for a festive meal.

Method

Combine apples, sugar, lemon juice, cinnamon, nutmeg, and salt in one bowl. In a separate bowl, create a crumbly mixture by combining flour, brown sugar, oats, and butter. Place the apple mixture in an oven-proof dish and top with the crumbly mixture. Cook in the air fryer at 180C/360F for 25 minutes or until apples are tender and the crumble is golden brown and crunchy.

Serves 4, Preparation time approx 30 mins, Cooking time approx 25 mins

Apple Pie

2 pre-made refrigerated pie crusts			Apples, peeled, diced	450 g	1 lb
Granulated Sugar	50 g	1/4 cup	Plain/all-purpose flour	15 g	2 tbsp
Ground cinnamon		2 tsp	Ground nutmeg		1/2 tsp
Salted butter, melted	15 g	1/2 oz	Brown sugar	50 g	1/4 cup
1 egg, beaten					

About

Apple pie has become a staple at Christmas celebrations. In many regions, apples are harvested in the late summer and early autumn, meaning they are plentiful and at their best during the holiday season, either fresh or stored. Apple pie is often associated with comfort and warmth, two feelings that are highly sought after during the Christmas season. An apple pie's sweet and slightly tart flavour profile pairs exceptionally well with other traditional Christmas foods.

Method

Line a baking dish with parchment paper and one pie crust. Mix apples, sugar, flour, cinnamon, and nutmeg in a bowl. Pour this mixture into the lined dish, drizzle with melted butter, and sprinkle brown sugar on top. Cover with the second pie crust, sealing and crimping the edges. Brush the top with the beaten egg. Cook in the air fryer at 180C/360F for 20 to 30 minutes or until the crust is golden and the filling is bubbling.

Serves 4, Preparation time approx 30 mins, Cooking time approx 30 mins

Bread Pudding

Cubed stale bread	350 g	5 cups	Milk	500 ml	2 cups
2 large eggs, beaten			Granulated sugar	90 g	1/2 cup
Salted butter, melted	30 ml	2 tbsp	Vanilla extract		1 tsp
Ground cinnamon		1/2 tsp	Sultanas or mixed dried fruit	90 g	1/2 cup
Spray oil					

About

The tradition has deep historical roots and varies from place to place. Bread pudding often appears during the festive season as part of a long-standing culinary tradition. December weather can be chilly in many parts of the world, and a warm, hearty dish like bread pudding is incredibly comforting. It's perfect for enjoying beside a roaring fire or as a satisfying end to a Christmas feast.

Method

Soak the bread cubes in the milk in a bowl for 10 minutes. Combine the eggs, sugar, melted butter, vanilla extract, dried fruits, and cinnamon in a separate bowl. After soaking, add the bread cubes to the egg mixture and stir to combine.

Pour the blended mixture into a deep, lightly oil-sprayed, round or square oven-proof dish or cake barrel which fits comfortably in your air fryer, and cook at 160C/320F in the air fryer for 30 minutes, stirring every 5 minutes. Remove it from the air fryer and let it set before serving it with warm custard or cream (optional)

Serves 4 to 6, Preparation time approx 30 mins, Cooking time approx 30 mins

Christmas Fruit Cake

Zest of 2 lemons			Black treacle, or molasses	30 ml	2 tbsp
Mixed dried fruit of choice	900 g	2 lb	Plain/all-purpose flour	240 g	2 cups
Unsalted butter	225 g	8 oz	Soft brown sugar	225 g	8 oz
5 eggs, beaten			Ground nutmeg		1/2 tsp
Sea salt		1/2 tsp	Brandy, or dark rum	60 ml	1/4 cup

About

The Christmas cake has a rich and diverse history, steeped in various traditions that have evolved over centuries. Its roots can be traced back to the Middle Ages when it was customary in parts of Europe to celebrate the winter season with a type of porridge. This festive dish was enhanced with spices, dried fruit, and honey.

Method

Mix and soak the dried fruit in the brandy in a covered bowl overnight. When ready to make the cake, drain the liquid from the bowl, discard it, and set the fruit aside. Blend the butter and sugar in a mixing bowl until they achieve a light and fluffy texture. Gradually incorporate the beaten eggs into this mixture. Next, gently fold in the flour and nutmeg. Once these are well combined, add the dried fruit, lemon zest, and treacle.

Transfer the prepared batter into a 20 cm/8-inch round or square cake tin or cake barrel that comfortably fits in your air fryer basket/tray/rack and is lined with parchment paper. Cover the tin with foil and cook in the air fryer at 130C/270F for one hour. After this, remove the foil and cook for 30 minutes until the cake turns golden brown and develops a firm crust. To confirm its doneness, insert a skewer into the middle of the cake; it should come out dry. After baking, set it aside to cool down before you decorate.

Serves 4 to 6, Preparation time approx 30 mins, Cooking time approx 1 hour 30 mins

Christmas Victoria Sponge

Self-raising/rising flour	225 g	1 3/4 cups	Unsalted butter, room temperature	225 g	8 oz
Caster sugar	225 g	1 cup	4 large eggs		
Baking powder		2 tsp	Vanilla extract		1 tsp
Sea salt		1/4 tsp	Cranberry sauce (to your liking)		
Prepared thick whipped cream (to your liking)			Ground cinamon		1/4 tsp
Allspice		1/4 tsp			

About

The Victoria Sponge, despite not being a traditional Christmas dessert, has garnered popularity during the Christmas season for several reasons. Named after Queen Victoria, who was said to enjoy a slice with her afternoon tea, the Victoria Sponge is a treat. Its simple yet decadent nature allows it to fit seamlessly into the array of more traditionally festive dishes.

Method

In a large bowl, combine butter and sugar until light and fluffy. Beat in eggs one by one, then add vanilla. Sift in flour, baking powder, and salt, and fold until combined. Distribute the batter between two parchment paper-lined 20 cm/8 inch cake tins, or once which fit your air fryer.

Cook at 180C/360F for 20 to 25 minutes, separately or on a trivet rack, until a skewer comes out clean from the centre. Let the cakes cool, then spread your desired amount of jam and whipped cream on one and sandwich with the other. Dust with flour.

Serves 4, Preparation time approx 30 mins, Cooking time approx 25 mins

Gingerbread Men

Ground cinnamon		1 tsp	Ground ginger		2 tsp
Plain/all-purpose flour	360 g	3 cups	Ground cloves		1/2 tsp
1 egg, beaten			Salted butter, melted	80 g	3 oz
Brown sugar	140 g	3/4 cup	Molasses, or maple syrup	125 ml	1/2 cup

About

Gingerbread has a long history, with its origins traced back to ancient civilisations. The ginger root was prized for its medicinal properties and eventually found its way into culinary applications, including spiced bread and cakes. The practice of shaping gingerbread into various forms is believed to have started in the 16th century. The association between gingerbread men and Christmas is a more recent tradition.

Method

First, melt the butter and blend it with the sugar, molasses, and egg until well combined. Next, incorporate the mixture of spices, including cinnamon, ginger, and cloves. Add flour to the wet ingredients and stir until the dough forms. If the dough is too sticky, add a little flour until you reach the desired consistency.

Once the dough is prepared, encase it in cling film/plastic wrap and chill in the freezer for approximately 10 minutes. After it has cooled, roll the dough to 1 cm / 1/4 inch thick and use biscuit/cookie cutters to shape it into gingerbread men or other shapes. Cook them in the air fryer basket/tray/rack at 180C/360F for 8 minutes or until golden brown. Decorate as you wish with icing sugar or leave without.

Serves 4 to 6, Preparation time approx 30 mins, Cooking time approx 8 mins

Lemon Drizzle Cake

Self-raising/rising flour	220 g	1 3/4 cups	3 eggs, beaten		
Caster sugar	170 g	3/4 cup	Freshly squeezed lemon juice	15 ml	1 tbsp
Zest of 1 lemon			**Drizzle**		
Milk	45 ml	3 tbsp	Caster sugar	20 g	2 tbsp
Salted butter	180 g	3/4 cup	Freshly squeezed lemon juice	30 ml	2 tbsp

About

Lemon drizzle cake has increasingly found a place in festive celebrations, while not traditionally associated with Christmas in the way that, say, mince pies or Christmas pudding are. The glistening lemon syrup or glaze can evoke a festivity reminiscent of snow or frost. Additionally, the cake can be decorated with Christmas-themed garnishes like holly or seasonal fruits to make it more holiday-appropriate.

Method

In a medium bowl, cream the butter and sugar until fluffy. Beat in the eggs individually, followed by lemon zest and juice. Gradually mix in the flour to form a soft dough. Line a 20 cm cake tin with parchment. Pour in the batter and bake in the air fryer at 160C/320F for 30 to 40 minutes or until golden and a skewer tested in the centre of the cake comes out clean.

Drizzle: Combine the sugar and lemon juice and brush it onto the cake once cooled.

Serves 4, Preparation time approx 30 mins, Cooking time approx 40 mins

Melting Moments

Unsalted butter, softened	120 g	4 oz	Caster sugar	50 g	1/4 cup
Vanilla extract	5 ml	1 tsp	Plain/all-purpose flour	170 g	1 1/2 cups
Cornflour/cornstarch	60 g	1/2 cup	Sea salt		1/4 tsp

About

Melting Moments are a delightful biscuit/cookie variety known for their tender, crumbly texture and rich, buttery flavour. Like many popular Christmas treats, Melting Moments are rich in butter, a staple ingredient during feasting seasons. The butter gives the biscuits/cookies their characteristic 'melt-in-the-mouth' quality and makes them feel indulgent, which is fitting for the spirit of abundance during the holidays.

Method

Cream the butter, vanilla, and sugar until fluffy in a large bowl. Sift in the flour, cornflour/cornstarch, and salt to form a dough. If it is too dry to create, add more butter. If it is too wet, add a little more flour. Roll the dough into biscuit/cookie-sized balls, remembering they should flatten out, place on a plate, and refrigerate for 30 minutes.

Cook in a single layer in a parchment paper-lined air fryer basket/tray/rack at 180C/360F for 10 to 12 minutes or until lightly golden. Optionally, sandwich two with jam or cream or top with a dollop of jam.

Serves 4, Preparation time approx 45 mins, Cooking time approx 12 mins

Mince Pies

Shortcrust pastry or buy 450 g/1 lb of ready-made					
Plain/all-purpose flour	180 g	1 1/2 cups	Pinch of sea salt		
Butter, cubed	80 g	3 oz	Cold water	30 ml	2 tbsp
Filling					
1 jar of mince pie mincemeat	400 g	14 oz	1 egg, beaten		
Icing sugar or plain/all-purpose flour for dusting					

About

Mince pies can trace their origins to medieval England. During this period, they were known as "shred pies" or "mutton pies" and were made with a mixture of finely chopped or shredded meat, such as mutton or beef, combined with fruits, spices, and suet. Fruits, particularly raisins, currants, and apples, took on a more prominent role, giving mince pies their sweet and fruity flavor.

Method

Shortcrust: In a large bowl, mix flour and salt, then add the cubed butter. Quickly rub in the butter until the mixture looks like coarse breadcrumbs. Add enough cold water, starting with 15 ml/1 tbsp, and stir to form a dough. Knead lightly until smooth, handle minimally to keep it tender, then wrap in cling film and refridgerate for 30 minutes.

Mince pies: Dust a worktop and rolling pin with flour. Roll out the pastry and, using cutters, shape it to the desired size. Place the pastry in individual muffin tins or several muffin tins which fit your air fryer. Spoon mincemeat into each. Cover with another layer of pastry, pressing or pinching the edges to seal the pies. Brush the tops with egg. Cook in the air fryer at 180C/360F for 15 minutes or until they are golden and cooked—dust with icing sugar or flour.

Serves 4 to 6, Preparation time approx 30 mins, Cooking time approx 15 mins

Nut Loaf

Walnuts, crushed	240 g	2 cups	Oat flour	60 g	1/2 cup
Almonds, crushed	120 g	1 cup	Ground cinnamon		1 tsp
Pecans, crushed	120 g	1 cup	Ground nutmeg		1/2 tsp
Grated/shredded coconut	90 g	1 cup	Ground ginger		1/2 tsp
Ground cloves		1/4 tsp	Maple syrup	30 ml	2 tbsp
Sea salt		1/2 tsp	Coconut oil, melted	30 ml	2 tbsp
Vanilla extract	5 ml	1 tsp	Spray oil		

About

A delightful alternative to the traditional meat-based centrepieces commonly found on British Christmas tables. The choice of nut loaf at Christmas can serve various purposes and hold different significance for different people. In winter, nuts are traditionally harvested and are, therefore, in season. Incorporating them into a nut loaf aligns well with using seasonal produce.

Method

Combine the walnuts, pecans, almonds, shredded coconut, flour, cinnamon, nutmeg, ginger, cloves, and salt in a bowl. Mix well. Whisk the maple syrup, coconut oil, and vanilla extract in another bowl. Pour wet ingredients into the dry ingredients and mix until combined. Spray oil or line a 20x10 cm / 8x4 inch loaf tin or one that will fit comfortably in your air fryer with parchment paper. Transfer the nut loaf batter to the tin and spread it evenly. Cook at 190C/370F for 25 minutes or until cooked to your liking.

Serves 4 to 6, Preparation time approx 30 mins, Cooking time approx 25 mins

Pavlova

2 large passionfruit			Whipping cream	250 ml	1 cup
1 mango, peeled, cored, and diced			White vinegar	5 ml	1 tsp
4 egg whites			Vanilla extract	5 ml	1 tsp
Caster sugar	225 g	1 cup	Cornflour/cornstarch		1 tsp

About

The Pavlova has become popular for Christmas celebrations, particularly in warmer countries such as Australia and New Zealand. The visual presentation, with its gleaming meringue and colourful fruit toppings, makes it a centrepiece-worthy addition. The vibrant colours add a touch of sophistication to Christmas celebrations.

Method

In a large bowl, use a blender or hand mixer to whisk egg whites until they form firm peaks. Gradually incorporate caster sugar, whisking until the mixture is thick and glossy. Slowly add cornflour, vinegar, and vanilla, beating well until thoroughly combined. Prepare your air fryer basket/tray/rack by lining it with parchment paper, which should also be lightly greased. Spoon the pavlova mixture onto the paper and gently flatten.

Set the air fryer to 120C/250F and bake for approximately 30 minutes, or until the pavlova is cooked to a marshmallow-like consistency. You don't need to worry about any cracks forming on the surface. Once the pavlova is firm, allow it to cool within the air fryer basket. The residual heat from the switched-off fryer will continue to cook it slightly. If your air fryer has a temperature setting as low as 90C/190F, continue cooking the pavlova at that temperature for a further half hour before removing it from the air fryer and allowing it cool. Serve with whipped cream and your choice of fruits, like passionfruit or mango pieces.

Serves 4, Preparation time approx 30 mins, Cooking time approx 30 mins to 1 hour.

Pecan Pie

Crust (if wanting to prepare your own crust, or use pre-made pastry dough)

Sea salt		1/4 tsp	Butter, room temperature	90 g	3 oz
Plain/all-purpose flour	150 g	1 1/4 cup	Warm water	60 ml	1/4 cup

Filling

Pecans, chopped or halved	200 g	1 1/2 cup	Light corn syrup or golden syrup	250 ml	1 cup
Brown sugar	180 g	1 cup	Vanilla extract	5 ml	1 tsp
Sea salt		1/2 tsp	4 eggs, beaten		

About

Originating in the southern United States, pecan pie has become a quintessential dessert worldwide. This dish features prominently in celebrations.

Method

Pie crust: For the crust, mix flour, salt, and butter until flaky. Add water by the tbsp until the dough is smooth. Roll out on a floured surface and fit into your pie tin.

Pecan pie: Choose a pie tin or dish that fits your air fryer and allows for good airflow. Prepare or use a premade pie dough and line the pie tin. Cook the crust in the air fryer at 150C/300F for 5 minutes, then set it aside.

Mix syrup, sugar, salt, butter, and vanilla in a bowl. Whisk eggs in another bowl; add to the mixture with pecans. Fill crust, cover with foil, and air fry at 180F/360F for 30 minutes. Remove the foil for 20 minutes and continue cooking. The pie is done when the crust is firm and the centre slightly jiggles. It sets upon cooling.

Serves 4 to 6, Preparation time approx 30 mins, Cooking time approx 30 mins

Pumpkin Pie

1 sheet of premade crust, large enough to line a 20 cm / 8 inch shallow pie tin or one which fits your air fryer					
Ground cinnamon		1/2 tsp	Heavy cream	125 ml	1/2 cup
Ground ginger		1/2 tsp	2 eggs, beaten		
Ground nutmeg		1/2 tsp	Granulated sugar	50 g	1/4 cup
Ground cloves		1/2 tsp	Brown sugar	40 g	1/4 cup
Pumpkin purée	250 ml	1 cup	Sea salt		1/4 tsp
Cornflour/cornstarch		2 tsp			

About

Pumpkin pie has also found its way into Christmas celebrations. Its roots can be traced back to early European recipes that used squashes and pumpkins. Today, pumpkin pie is enjoyed throughout the holiday season, including Thanksgiving and Christmas.

Method

Line the pie tin with a sheet of premade pie crust and chill it in the fridge for 30 minutes. While the crust is chilling, combine and blend the remaining ingredients in a mixing bowl using either a hand mixer or a whisk.

Take the tin out of the fridge, lightly fork-prick its base, and pour in the pie filling. Cook the pie at 180C/360F for 10 minutes. Reduce the temperatures to 160C/320F and cook for 20 minutes until the filling is firm on the surface and jiggles a little in the centre. Allow to cool before slicing and serving.

Serves 4 to 6, Preparation time approx 30 mins, Cooking time approx 30 mins

Pumpkin Shakarparas

Pumpkin purée	175 ml	3/4 cup	Semolina flour or wheat middling	60 g	1/2 cup
Plain/all-purpose flour	240 g	2 cups	Granulated sugar	150 g	3/4 cup
Baking powder		1 tsp	Pumpkin spice		1 tbsp
Ground cloves		1 tsp	Warm milk	60 ml	1/2 cup
Unsalted butter	15 g	1/2 oz	1 egg, beaten		

About

If you want to diversify your Christmas treats or incorporate a fusion element, Pumpkin Shakarparas could be an exciting choice. They could serve as a unique and multicultural addition to the range of cookies, cakes, and other sweet treats on the Christmas table.

Method

Combine the flour, semolina flour, baking powder, pumpkin spice, and ground cloves in a large mixing bowl. Next, blend in all the wet ingredients, excluding the milk, which will be used to form the dough. Gradually add the warmed milk, mixing continuously to achieve a somewhat firm yet smooth dough.

Knead the mixture for approximately 10 minutes. Divide the dough into four equal parts on a floured surface. Using a rolling pin, flatten each portion into a large circle about 3 mm / 1/8 inch thick. Cut the dough into long strips of 1.3 cm / 1/2-inch width using a sharp knife or pizza cutter. Then, cut these strips across the other way to form squares or diamond-shaped pieces.

Cook the shakarparas in a single layer in the air fryer basket/tray/rack at 190C/370F for about 6 minutes or until golden brown, adjusting the time based on the size of the pieces. Allow them to cool for 5 minutes before serving.

Serves 4 to 6, Preparation time approx 30 mins, Cooking time approx 6 mins

Roasted Mixed Nuts

Honey	15 ml	1 tbsp	Hot sauce of choice (optional)	5 ml	1 tsp
Smoked paprika		1/2 tsp	Sea salt		1/2 tsp
Olive oil	15 ml	1 tbsp	Unsalted almonds	70 g	1/2 cup
Unsalted cashew nuts	70 g	1/2 cup	Unsalted peanuts	70 g	1/2 cup
Unsalted hazelnuts	70 g	1/2 cup	Ground black pepper		1/4 tsp
Optionally, replace any of the above nuts, or add other nuts of choice					

About

Nuts have often been seen as symbols of rebirth and renewal. The hard shell encapsulating the life within can be viewed as a metaphor for the cradle of the infant Jesus, making nuts appropriate for Christian Christmas traditions.

Method

In a large bowl, combine oil, honey, hot sauce (optional), paprika, and salt and pepper. Add the nuts. Stir the nuts into the mixture until all the nuts are thoroughly coated.

Cook the nuts in a single layer of parchment paper in the air fryer basket/tray/rack at 150C/300F for 10 minutes, stirring halfway to ensure even roasting. Once done, transfer the nuts to a plate to cool. Once cooled, them into clusters if they have stuck together.

Serves 4 to 6, Preparation time approx 30 mins, Cooking time approx 10 mins

Scones

Vanilla extract		1/2 tsp	Freshly squeezed lemon juice	5 ml	1 tsp
Milk	80 ml	1/3 cup	Caster sugar	20 g	2 tbsp
Milk (for glazing)	15 ml	1 tbsp	Unsalted butter, cubed	45 g	1 1/2 oz
Baking powder		1/2 tsp	Self-raising/rising flour	180 g	1 1/2 cups

About

While scones are not a traditional Christmas treat per se, they can be a delightful addition to your holiday spread by slicing them in half and incorporating seasonal ingredients. Think cranberry and orange scones or spiced gingerbread scones, and dd clotted or extra thick cream.

Method

Combine the flour, baking powder, and cubed butter in a large bowl until crumbly. Add caster sugar. Warm the 80 ml / 1/3 cup of milk in a saucepan, or microwave it for 30 seconds, and stir in lemon juice and vanilla. Let it stand for 3 minutes, then mix it into the mixed ingredients in the bowl to form a sticky dough.

On a floured surface, shape the dough into a 2.5 cm/1 inch thick disc and cut out five scones using a 5 cm/2 inch cutter. Re-form and use any remaining dough to make more scones. Glaze the scones with a little of the 15 ml/1 tbsp of milk. Cook in the air fryer basket at 180C/360F for 10 minutes or until golden. Cool on a wire rack for 10 minutes before serving. Optionally, slice in half and insert Christmas-related ingredients, such as clotted cream and cranberry sauce, sprinkle with flour, icing sugar, or decorate.

Serves 4 to 6, Preparation time approx 30 mins, Cooking time approx 10 mins

Shortbread Biscuits/Cookies

Plain/all-purpose flour	240 g	2 cups	Unsalted butter, softened	100 g	3 1/2 oz
Granulated sugar	50 g	1/4 cup	Sea salt		1/4 tsp
Turbinado, or demerara sugar	20 g	2 tbsp			

About

Shortbread has a rich history that lends itself to being enjoyed during the festive Christmas season. Shortbread was initially derived from medieval biscuit bread. Over time, the yeast was replaced with butter, which was a luxury item. This luxurious nature of shortbread made it suitable for special occasions, and it became associated with Christmas and New Year's celebrations, particularly Hogmanay in Scotland.

Method

Combine the flour, butter, sugar, and salt in a medium bowl. Knead it until a dough forms. Flatten the dough to about 1.3 cm / 1/2 inch thick, use a shape cutter to create the shapes you wish, and add patterns with the back of a knife or other utensils. Sprinkle with demerara or turbinado sugar and cook in the air fryer basket/tray/rack on parchment paper at 180C/360F for 8 to 10 minutes or until lightly golden and cooked. Cool on a wire rack.

Serves 4 to 6, Preparation time approx 30 mins, Cooking time approx 10 mins

Sugar Cookies/Biscuits

Vanilla extract	5 ml	1 tsp	2 eggs, beaten		
Granulated sugar	200 g	1 cup	Unsalted butter, room temperature	240 g	8 1/2 oz
Sea salt		1/2 tsp	Baking powder		1 tsp
Plain/all-purpose flour	240 g	2 cups			

About

The origins of the sugar cookie can be traced back to the 1700s in Nazareth, Pennsylvania when German Protestant settlers created the "Nazareth Cookie". Over time, as recipes were handed down through generations, baking sugar cookies became a holiday tradition in many families. They are often left out for Santa Claus on Christmas Eve, further embedding them in Christmas lore.

Method

In a medium bowl, combine flour, baking powder, and salt. In a mixer bowl or a bowl with a hand mixer, cream the butter for about a minute. Introduce the sugar and beat gently until light and fluffy. Incorporate the egg and vanilla, beating until combined. Gradually add the flour mixture, mixing gently. Chill the dough in the fridge for 30 minutes.

Shape the dough into balls and press them flat using a glass base or rolling pin. Line the air fryer basket/tray/rack with parchment paper and cook the cookies/biscuits, ensuring ample space between each as they expand, at 160C/320F for 8 minutes or until golden. Allow them to cool on the parchment paper.

Serves 4 to 6, Preparation time approx 30 mins, Cooking time approx 8 mins

Sweet Almonds

Ground cinnamon		1 tsp	Sea salt		1/2 tsp
Brown sugar	50 g	1/3 cup	Granulated sugar	60 g	1/3 cup
Raw almonds	250 g	2 cups	Vanilla extract	5 ml	1 tsp
2 egg whites			Toasted sesame seeds or other		1 tbsp

About

The tradition of enjoying nuts, including almonds, during Christmas dates back centuries and spans multiple cultures. Nuts are often associated with prosperity and good fortune, making them suitable for celebrations.

Method

Whisk the egg white in a large mixing bowl until it turns frothy, then incorporate the vanilla. Gently mix in the almonds to coat them and seeds. Blend the sugar, salt, and cinnamon in a bowl. Add this dry mixture to the almonds and stir until evenly coated.

Cook the almonds in a single layer in a parchment paper-lined air fryer basket/tray/rack. Cook at 150C/300F for 25 minutes or until the almonds crisp. Once cooled, store the candied almonds in a sealed container to maintain freshness.

Serves 4, Preparation time approx 30 mins, Cooking time approx 25 mins

Sweet Pecans

Sea salt		1/4 tsp	Pecan halves	300 g	2 cups
Ground cinnamon		1 tsp	Ground ginger		1/2 tsp
Ground nutmeg		1/4 tsp	Maple syrup	15 ml	1 tbsp
Water	15 ml	1 tbsp	Ground cardamom		1/2 tsp

About

Pecan harvest season typically falls in late autumn. This makes them readily available and fresh during the Christmas season. Pecans feature prominently in several traditional Christmas recipes, such as pecan pie, and their rich, buttery flavour complements the sweet and spiced profiles commonly associated with holiday fare.

Method

Line the air fryer basket with parchment paper. In a large bowl, combine all the ingredients in a medium-sized bowl and toss until they are thoroughly coated.

Cook the coated pecans in the air fryer basket/tray/rack at 170C/340F for 8 minutes or until they shine and smell delicious. Shake the basket halfway through the cooking time.

Lay out a sheet of parchment paper and evenly spread the pecans on the sheet, allowing them to cool for 30 minutes before serving.

Serves 4 to 6, Preparation time approx 30 mins, Cooking time approx 8 mins

Apple Sauce

Great with: Pork, vegetables, desserts

6 apples, a mix of different varieties if possible		
Water	250 ml	1 cup
Granulated sugar	60 g	1/3 cup
Ground cinnamon		1 tsp

Method

Peel, core, and slice the apples, then mix them with the water, sugar, and cinnamon in a saucepan. Cook covered on medium heat until the apples soften, which might take about 20 minutes.

Let the mixture cool down, then mash to your desired consistency using a fork or a potato masher.

Serves 6

Bechamel Sauce

Great with: Pasta, seafood, vegetables

Parmesan cheese, grated/shredded	10 g	1 tbsp
Ground nutmeg		1/4 tsp
Milk	500 ml	2 cups
Unsalted butter	60 g	2 oz
Plain/all-purpose flour	60 g	1/2 cup
Pinch of sea salt		

Method

Melt the butter in a medium saucepan over low heat and sift in the flour to avoid lumps. Swiftly blend the ingredients using a whisk until smooth. Warm the milk in a separate saucepan and pour it into the butter-flour mixture, combining thoroughly for 2 minutes. Remove from the heat.

Allow the mixture to go warm before seasoning. Add a pinch of salt, nutmeg, and Parmesan cheese and stir well.

Serves 6 to 8

Bread Sauce

Great with: Chicken, turkey, other poultry

White bread without crusts, torn	120 g	4 oz
2 bay leaves		
4 cloves		
1 small onion, peeled, sliced		
Ground nutmeg		1/4 tsp
10 peppercorns		
Sea salt		1/4 tsp
Milk	500 ml	2 cups

Method

Place milk, onion, clove, bay leaves, pepper, and nutmeg in a small saucepan and warm over low heat until almost boiling, then turn off the heat, cover the saucepan and let the milk infuse with the added flavours for 30 minutes.

Afterwards, discard the solids and strain the infused milk through a sieve into a fresh saucepan. Add the torn bread and salt to the strained milk. Bring the mixture to a boil and then reduce the heat to a gentle simmer. Continue simmering until the bread sauce reaches your desired thickness.

Serves 4 to 6

Cheese Sauce

Great with: Steak, vegetables, savouries

Mature cheddar, grated/shredded	120 g	4 oz
Unsalted butter	60 g	2 oz
Plain/all-purpose flour	30 g	1/4 cup
Full-fat milk	400 ml	1 1/2 cups

Method

Combine the milk, flour, and butter in a saucepan. Place the saucepan over medium heat and whisk vigorously.

Continue whisking as the butter melts, the flour dissolves, and the mixture as it comes to a boil. Once at a boil, keep whisking for a couple of minutes.

Finally, incorporate the grated/shredded mature cheddar cheese until it melts into the mixture. If the sauce is too thick for your liking, add a little more milk. If it is too thin, add more flour or cheese and mix well.

Serves 4 to 6

Cranberry Sauce

Great with: All meats, veg dishes and desserts

Fresh or frozen cranberries	450 g	1 lb
Zest and juice of 1 orange		
Caster sugar	60 g	1/3 cup
Port, or sherry. Sherry is sweeter	30 ml	2 tbsp

Method

Combine cranberries, port or sherry, and the zest and juice of the orange in a saucepan over medium heat. Bring the mixture to a boil before lowering the heat to let it simmer. Stir until the cranberries start to soften.

Incorporate the sugar and transfer the mixture to a serving dish. Allow it to cool to room temperature before serving.

Serves 4 to 6

Diane Sauce

Great with: all meats and vegetables

Olive oil	10 ml	2 tsp
Salted butter	30 g	1 oz
1 small onion, peeled, finely chopped		
Ground black pepper		1/4 tsp
1 garlic glove, grated/shredded		
Cognac or brandy	30 ml	2 tbsp
Beef broth or stock	200 ml	3/4 cup
Dijon mustard	15 ml	1 tbsp
Heavy or double cream	125 ml	1/2 cup
Worcestershire sauce	5 ml	1 tsp

Method

Melt the butter with the oil over medium heat in a frying pan/skillet. Add the onion, pepper, garlic, and sauté until the onion softens. Introduce the cognac or brandy and let the mixture bubble for 1 minute.

Add the broth or stock, Worcestershire sauce, and mustard, and continue to cook until the mixture has thickened. Incorporate the cream and, if you have them, add up to 30 ml/2 tbsp of meat juices. Bring the mixture to a simmer before removing from heat.

Serves 6

Horseradish Cream

Great with: All meats, cooked veg or salads

Prepared horseradish sauce	30 ml	2 tbsp
Soured/sour cream	125 ml	1/2 cup
Apple cider vinegar	5 ml	1 tsp
Mayonnnaise	30 ml	2 tbsp
Pinch of sea salt and black pepper		1/4 tsp
Chives, finely chopped		1 tbsp

Method

Mix all the ingredients together in a small bowl. You may serve it immediately or store it in a covered container in the fridge for up to one week.

Serves 4

Lemon Garlic Butter

Great with: Fish, other meats and vegetables

Sea salt and black pepper to taste		
Fresh parsley, finely chopped		1 tsp
Zest and juice of 1 lemon		
4 garlic cloves, grated/shredded		
Unsalted butter	90 g	3 oz
Olive oil	60 ml	1/4 cup

Method

Add the olive oil over medium heat in a small saucepan until hot. Add the garlic and sauté it for 1 minute. Add the butter and melt it into the oil and garlic.

Once melted and combined, remove the pan from the heat and stir in the lemon zest, juice, and parsley. Add salt and pepper according to your preference.

Serves 2 to 4

Mint Sauce

Great with: Lamb, other meats, vegetables

Fresh mint leaves and tender stalks	225 g	8 oz
Brown sugar	60 g	1/3 cup
White wine vinegar	30 ml	2 tbsp
Fresh sage, finely chopped		2 tsp

Method

Rinse the mint leaves thoroughly and remove any thick or tough stalks. Finely chop the mint, place it in a bowl with the sage and mix in 15 ml/1 tbsp of vinegar to achieve a thick consistency. Add vinegar until you reach your desired thickness; the sauce should hold its shape without appearing watery.

Add a few teaspoons of sugar at a time and mix well. Add sugar and vinegar and mix until satisfied with the flavour and texture. Once happy, refrigerate the sauce for at least 4 hours before serving. Store any leftover sauce in an airtight container for two weeks.

Serves 4 to 6

Salted Caramel Sauce

Great with: Desserts

Salted butter	60 g	2 oz
Water	125 ml	1/2 cup
Heavy or whipping cream	125 ml	1/2 cup
Granulated sugar	200 g	1 cup
Vanilla extract		1/2 tsp
Pinch of sea salt to taste		

Method

In a medium saucepan, dissolve the sugar in the water over medium-low heat. Add the butter and melt it in. Increase to medium heat and bring to a boil. Avoid whisking at this stage to prevent crystallisation. Boil until it turns a deep golden colour without stirring, but occasionally swirling the saucepan for even cooking. Remove from the heat.

Off the heat, add the heavy or whipping cream while whisking vigorously. Stir in the vanilla and a pinch of salt to taste. Allow the sauce to cool; it will thicken as it does. Store refrigerated for up to two weeks.

Serves 4 to 6

Seafood Sauce

Great with: Prawns/shrimps, seafood, salad

Hot sauce of choice		1/2 tsp
Freshly squeezed lemon juice	15 ml	1 tbsp
Tomato ketchup	15 ml	1 tbsp
Paprika		1/2 tsp
Mayonnaise	125 ml	1/2 cup
Garlic powder		1/4 tsp
Worcestershire sauce	5 ml	1 tsp

Method

Place all ingredients in a mixing bowl or food processor and blend to a smooth sauce.

Serves 2 to 4

Beef Gravy

Great with: Roasts, steaks, other beef dishes

Beef broth or stock	750 ml	3 cups
1 beef stock cube or 5 ml/1 tsp liquid bouillon		
Butter	60 g	2 oz
Sea salt and black pepper to taste		
Garlic powder		1/2 tsp
Onion powder		1/2 tsp
Plain/all-purpose flour	60 g	1/2 cup

Method

Over medium heat, combine the butter and flour in a saucepan, stirring consistently to create a roux (thickener). Gradually introduce half of the beef broth or stock, whisking briskly to ensure a smooth, lump-free mixture.

Then, add the remaining beef broth with onion powder, garlic powder, and beef stock cube or bouillon. Allow the gravy to boil until it achieves a thick and smooth consistency. Finally, adjust the seasoning with salt and pepper to taste.

Serves 6 to 8

Easy Gravy

Great with: Use stocks of choice

Broth or stock, flavour of choice	750 ml	3 cups
Plain/all-purpose flour	40 g	1/3 cup
Butter	60 g	2 oz
Ground black pepper		1/4 tsp
Sea salt to taste		

Method

Melt the butter in a saucepan over medium heat. Whisk in the flour, add the pepper, and cook until golden brown. The hue will deepen the longer it cooks. Gradually add broth or stock, continuously whisking to blend the ingredients smoothly.

Keep cooking and stirring until the mixture reaches your preferred consistency. Take the saucepan off the heat and season with salt to your liking.

Serves 6 to 8

KFC-Style Gravy

Great with: Chicken and other poultry

White pepper		1/4 tsp
1 beef stock cube or 1 tsp bouillon		
Unsalted butter	60 g	2 oz
1 chicken stock cube or 1 tsp bouillon		
Water	500 ml	2 cups
Plain/all-purpose flour	30 g	1/4 cup
Onion powder		1/2 tsp

Method

Melt butter over medium heat in a saucepan and blend in flour, onion powder, and pepper using a wooden spoon or whisk. Boil the water in a saucepan or kettle and dilute the stock cube or bouillon in the water by stirring.

Gradually introduce half the hot liquid to the flour and butter mixture, stirring continuously. Add the remaining liquid upon thickening and continue to stir until the mixture attains a gravy-like consistency. Adjust the seasoning with additional salt and pepper if required.

Serves 4 to 6

Mushroom Gravy

Great with: Beef, pork, poultry, vegetarian

Vegetable broth or stock	750 ml	3 cups
1 onion, peeled, finely chopped		
Cremini or white mushrooms, sliced	450 g	1 lb
Tamari sauce	10 ml	2 tsp
1 garlic clove, grated/shredded		
Plain/all-purpose flour	30 g	1/4 cup
Fresh parsley, finely chopped		1 tbsp
Sea salt and ground pepper to taste		
Olive oil	30 ml	2 tbsp

Method

Warm the olive oil over medium heat in a large frying pan/skillet. Sauté the onion until tender. Add the mushrooms and continue cooking until they soften. Add tamari, garlic, and parsley to the mixture, followed by sprinkling over the flour. Stir consistently for about a minute.

Pour in the broth and allow the mixture to simmer until it thickens, whisking frequently. This could take some time. Finalise by seasoning with salt and pepper to taste.

6 to 8

Onion Gravy

Great with: Beef, pork, poultry

Sea salt and black pepper to taste		
Worcestershire sauce	30 ml	2 tbsp
Olive oil	15 ml	1 tbsp
2 onions, peeled, sliced		
Dried thyme		1/2 tsp
Dijon mustard	5 ml	1 tsp
Beef broth or stock	400	1 1/2 cup
Plain/all-purpose flour	8 g	1 tbsp

Method

Warm the oil over low heat in a saucepan and sauté the onions until they soften.

Increase the heat to medium add a little of the broth or stock and stir in the flour. Gradually introduce the beef broth or stock while continually stirring. Incorporate mustard, thyme, Worcestershire sauce, and season with salt and pepper. Allow the mixture to simmer until it reaches your desired consistency.

2 to 4

Pork Gravy
Great with: Roast pork, other pork dishes

2 garlic cloves, chopped		
Sea salt and black pepper to taste		
2 pork stock cubes or 2 tsp bouillon		
Water	60 ml	1/4 cup
Plain/all-purpose flour	30 g	1/4 cup
Low-sodium chicken broth or stock	500 ml	2 cups
Unsalted butter	60 g	2 oz
1 onion, peeled, chopped		

Method

Add butter, garlic, and onion to a saucepan over medium heat, stirring to achieve some browning. Incorporate the flour with a whisk and cook and whisk the mixture until browned.

Gradually whisk in the chicken stock or broth, stock cubes or bouillon, ensuring a smooth consistency and bring the mixture to a simmer, stirring regularly.

Once it's been thickened to your liking, you can season with salt and pepper.

Serves 4 to 6

Turkey Gravy
Great with: Roast turkey, poultry dishes

Fresh herbs, finely chopped	5 g	1 tbsp
Turkey broth or stock	500 ml	2 cups
Cornflour/cornstarch	40 g	1/3 cup
Water	80 ml	1/3 cup

Method

Combine water with cornflour/cornstarch to create a thick mixture/slurry.

Heat the stock in a saucepan. Gradually whisk the cornflour/cornstarch mixture into the boiling stock to thicken it, adding as much as needed to achieve your preferred consistency.

Once thickened, incorporate fresh herbs and season with salt and pepper to taste before serving. If it becomes too thick, add water or stock and stir well.

Serves 4 to 6

Vegan & Gluten Free
Great with: all vegan dishes

Dijon mustard	5 ml	1 tsp
1 small onion, grated/shredded		
Tamari sauce	15 ml	1 tbsp
Rice flour	30 g	1/4 cup
Nutritional Yeast	30 g	3 tbsp
Vegetable broth or stock	500 ml	2 cups

Method

Combine all the ingredients in a medium-sized saucepan and bring the mixture to a boil. Whisk for a few minutes over medium-high heat until the gravy reaches your desired thickness. It can be stored in a sealed container in the fridge for up to a week.

Serves 4 to 6

Vegetable Gravy
Great with: cooked vegetables

1/2 onion, peeled, grated/shredded		
1 garlic clove, grated/shredded		
Pinch of sea salt and black pepper		
Butter	60 g	2 oz
Vegetable broth or stock	500 ml	2 cups
Plain/all-purpose flour	30 g	1/4 cup

Method

In a saucepan over medium heat, melt the butter and sauté the onion until it softens and takes on a light brown hue. Stir in the garlic and cook for an additional minute. Incorporate the flour, whisking continuously to eliminate any lumps, and cook for a further minute.

Gradually add the broth or stock, consistently whisking. Add the salt and pepper, continuing to whisk. Reduce to a simmer, stirring until you achieve your preferred gravy consistency.

Serves 4 to 6

Notes & Recipes

Notes & Recipes

Books To Look Out For

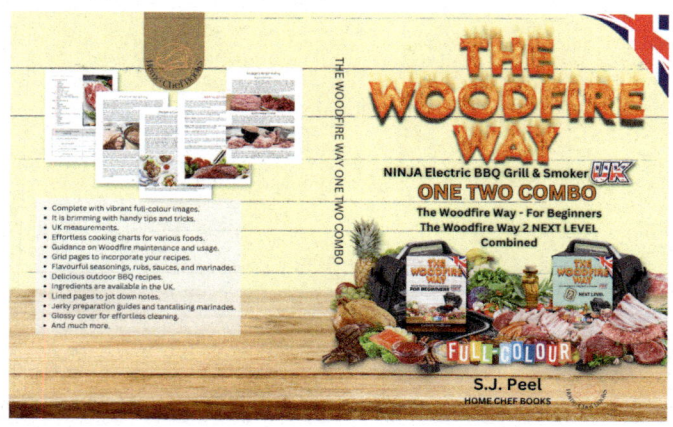

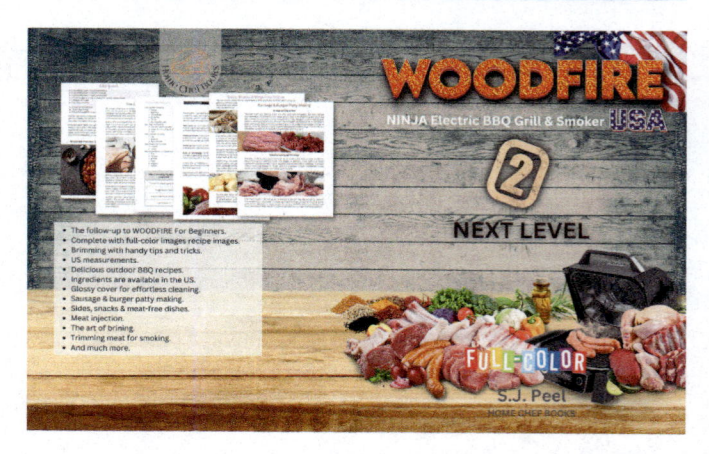

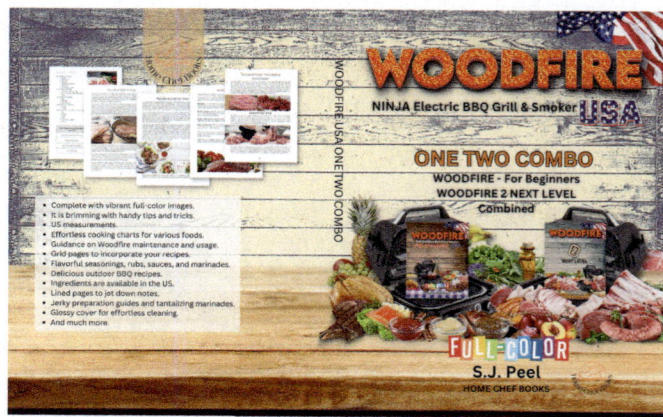

www.homechefbooks.com